Contagious COURAGE

Living in Freedom

VAHEN KING

Vern & Lois
Phil. 1:3.
Vahen K

CONTAGIOUS COURAGE

Copyright © 2021 by Vahen King

Published 2021 by GoingFarther.org

www.goingfarther.org

Cover photo: Vaughan King

Cover design: Shareen Baker

Cover and interior production: Vaughan King

Softcover ISBN: 978-0-9950909-5-8

E-book ISBN: 978-0-9950909-6-5

Cataloguing data available from Library and Archives Canada

Digital Printing in Canada by PageMaster Publishing

Table of Contents

Endorsements vii

Foreword xix

Introduction xxi

Section 1   Courage Is Possible! **1**

Chapter 1   Where to Begin When You're Building Again   3
Chapter 2   CTRL-Z   13
Chapter 3   Recycled Pain   23
Chapter 4   Where Does This Fit?   31

Section 2   Preparing for a Life of Courage **37**

Chapter 5   I Am Courageous!   39
Chapter 6   Knowing is Only Half the Battle   51
Chapter 7   Who Told You That?   59
Chapter 8   What's Stopping You?   69

Section 3   Courage To Grow... **81**

Chapter 9   Win The Day   83
Chapter 10   Grow Through What You Go Through   95
Chapter 11   What Does Your Fruit Taste Like? 103

Section 4   The Cost of Courage **123**

Chapter 12   What Are you Seeking? 125
Chapter 13   What's Your Muster Point? 131
Chapter 14   Keeping in Step 137

Table of Contents - page 2

Section 5   A Courageous Perspective *149*

Chapter 15   There's Always Another Way *151*
Chapter 16   You Can Make Extraordinary Ordinary! *157*
Chapter 17   A Reboot Changes Everything *163*

Section 6   A Life of Contagious Courage *169*

Chapter 18   What's Your New Normal? *171*
Chapter 19   The Strength of My Weakness *177*
Chapter 20   A Courageous Prayer of Blessing *183*
Chapter 21   Igniting Hearts With Hope *193*
Chapter 22   Rise and Shine *199*

Section 7   Reflect & Review *205*

Chapter 23   Your Courage Assessment *207*
Chapter 24   Battle For Endurance *223*

Resources *227*

Acknowledgments *231*

Special Thanks *235*

About The Author *239*

Dedication

Do you desire more for your life but are being held back by fears and insecurities? Whether you're a leader who's been strong in your faith for years, or you have never even considered God as an option, or somewhere in between, this book is dedicated to you. You who are facing impossible challenges, maybe even struggling to find hope, I wrote this book with you in mind.

It doesn't matter who you are, what position you hold, what race or religion you are, or what physical abilities you have, you are not exempt from the tragedies of loss and the negative side effects that threaten your freedom.

Come as you are, take off your mask, open your heart and start moving forward in freedom. Contagious Courage is dedicated to you. May you know you are worthy! Believe you are enough! And feel you are loved!

Endorsements

In a time where we are conditioned by social media to only write about the perfect times in our lives, Vahen's willingness to expose the faults and the flaws is like a breath of fresh air. As a result, it is relatable no matter what you are going through. Vahen King is remarkable and is a true inspiration for all of us. She could have focused on the highlights like being courageous enough to jump out of a plane or being Miss Wheelchair Canada. Both of those are amazing accomplishments. But instead, she showed us the valleys that she went through along the way. Being the amazing person that she is, Vahen has turned the diagnosis of transverse myelitis into a positive. But that road wasn't easy as *Contagious Courage* illustrates. She uses humility and humour to share her story and challenges the reader to "grow through what you go through."

You may be like me and you are thinking you aren't courageous in any way. *Contagious Courage* will challenge your thinking and help you change that mindset. Remove the blinders and see the truth about yourself. Vahen is living proof that God uses broken people to do amazing things. Trusting God and walking in faith will give you courage to face whatever circumstance you are going through. So, get ready to go farther in your journey by reading *Contagious Courage*.

Heather Whitehead
Ontario College Advanced Diploma (OCAD) Biotechnology,
Bachelor of Art (Honours) (BA) Psychology. Personal friend of Vahen King

Contagious Courage is going to be a great tool and an inspiration for so many. Because of Vahen's "never give up, never back down" attitude, she takes away the millions of excuses that people have about why they can't do X, Y or Z. Each person who reads *Contagious Courage* will come face to face with the challenge to take the next step. Imagine if millions of people had contagious courage—that's what I see happening as a result Vahen's book, *Contagious Courage*.

Jeremiah Raible
Certified Coach, Trainer and Speaker at The John Maxwell Team
Effectiveness Coach at ABNWT District PAOC

To see the impact of contagious courage we need look no farther than Mrs. Vahen King. *Contagious Courage* I believe is a must read for anyone interested in turning their troubles into triumphs.

Vahen bears her heart and soul in sharing the pain of her struggle with personal failure and of having to face the crippling disease which left her wheelchair-bound. But, Vahen shares her brokenness with one purpose in mind: to chart a pathway to hope—to show us how she transformed her troubles into triumphs and found defiant joy in the midst of life's difficulties.

Vahen has a dream to set the captives free – to free us all from whatever holds us back from following our dreams and living a life of unshakable faith – knowing that with God all things are possible.

Contagious Courage will touch your heart and change your life.

James H. Brown
James H. Brown & Associates - A personal injury law firm
Friend

Vahen King knows courage! And, she is no stranger to the challenges that require her to lean into her God as her strength and her confidence. Vahen describes herself as "confidently imperfect" and shares about her "defiant joy." These descriptions are never intended to place her above others but rather to call all of us higher. In this, her second book, Vahen takes us not just "behind the scenes" but into the interior working of the Lord in her heart. She chooses to have a conversation with the reader and even asks probing questions. Keep your pen ready to journal your responses!

I have favourite lines in the book such as when Vahen declares that her wheelchair is a platform of hope for others. She skillfully links that word "courage" with "contagious," and challenges us all to *"grow higher."* Welcome to the book. Welcome to the journey.

Peggy Kennedy
Speaker and Author
A is for Apple, Hear the Sound, Chosen
www.TwoSilverTrumpets.ca
"Contagious courage" sums up Vahen King in two words!

A sudden diagnosis of transverse myelitis just prior to her marriage could have destroyed Vahen. But it didn't. Facing the harsh reality of life in a wheelchair could have killed her dreams and calling. But it didn't.

Contagious Courage is Vahen's story. It chronicles many details of courage that rose in her spirit to break through many levels of pain, crisis, and fear into freedom. It was only divine empowerment that helped Vahen ditch the "I can't" mentality and to fully embrace a divine life-transforming truth: "I can do all things through Christ who strengthens me."

Meet Vahen and you have met sunshine, warmth, energy, and a zest for life. She glows with joy. Watch her quickly maneuver her wheelchair to her vehicle and lift herself into the driver's seat with one bounce of energy—and one must acknowledge a miracle. Hear her speak before an audience with words that are authentic and powerful—penetrating deeply into hearts. Listeners leave her presence determined to choose courage.

Being crowned Miss Wheelchair Canada in 2017 was the beginning of her becoming a voice of hope in our nation and beyond. Is there more ahead for Vahen King? Yes! Her contagious courage makes her unstoppable.

A must-read – a book needed today to ignite the power of courage and hope.

Margaret Gibb
Founder and Executive Director: Women Together
General Editor: Faith, Life & Leadership: 8 Canadian Women Tell Their Stories

I thoroughly enjoyed reading Vahen's book. I highly recommend it for anyone who feels a call for full-time ministry on their life as well as for those who desire more but are being held back by feeling they don't have the experience, education, correct background, or perfect faith. Vahen uses her own story to teach her readers to move past their failures and insecurities toward their God-given destiny. By asking her readers probing questions, she invites them to think through their fears and encourages them to step out in faith. Reading this book is like "holding a life coach in your hands."

Sheila Stauffer R.S.W.
Executive Director - Cornerstone Counselling

Vahen guides the reader through deeply moving autobiographical vignettes of how she triumphed over being diagnosed with Transverse Myelitis. Paralyzed from the chest down just after college graduation, she faced insurmountable struggles. Her inspirational story is one of victory. Using reflections on biblical characters and selected scriptures, she helps people work through the pain of disappointment and heartache. Time and again, Vahen exhorts us to never stop praying because prayer is "the key ingredient" in the Christian life. I think of her as Canada's Joni Eareckson Tada. Her book will be a blessing to you.

Garry E. Milley
BA(Ed), MTS, MA, DMin
Retired Professor and Pastor
Author: *Prophetic Voice in an Age of Upheaval, An Inconvenient Cross: Proclaiming Christ Crucified, Seven Shades of Sin: Unmasking Temptation*

Contagious Courage is packed full of inspirational stories. In one after another Vahen describes how the unexpected hardships in life don't have to hold you back from unexpected opportunities and blessings.

Authentic, open, real, and sometimes even raw personal stories help us identify those parts of our own lives that we may have falsely concluded will keep us bound. Too many of us hide amidst the barriers of our brokenness. Vahen offers us a pathway to find the courage to break through our fears and failures to go farther!

This book's pages are coloured with day-by-day, moment-by-moment open conversations with God. We often underestimate the power and strength that come from this simple but purposeful practice. Vahen's articulation of her "naturally supernatural" relationship with Jesus will motivate you to deepen your personal walk with God and energize you to climb new mountains by faith!

Rev. Kevin Shepherd
CEO | Crossroads, YES TV

"God recycles our pain." This is a phrase that rings loud for me long after I've read the last chapter. Vahen's story of contagious courage did not come easy. As I watched her struggle through her disability, insecurities, and low self esteem, I felt so helpless.

I turned to the only source of help I knew I could depend on. The only One I knew could recycle the mess of our lives. My heavenly Father. I prayed and asked others to join me and believe for her restoration.

It was in that desperate state that God showed me that Vahen was coming up out of the desert leaning on her beloved. (Song of Solomon 8:5) That was the key: *leaning.* Vahen did indeed come up and it wasn't by accessing her own strength but rather by clinging to His. The more she relied on God the more courageous she became.

I believe *Contagious Courage* is a very timely tool to put in the hands of our leaders. Vahen's message of how we can access God's strength to minister through pain rather than in the absence of it is very powerful. But even more than that, she shows us we can even experience joy in spite of overwhelming circumstances that would otherwise threaten to hold us back.

As a mother reading this book and thinking of the journey that we have been through together, I have a message for other parents who may have a heartbreaking story of your own. If you are struggling and watching your child suffer, you can trust God. Let Him recycle your pain. He will make something beautiful. And as Vahen acknowledges in the last chapter: "Remember, prayer is the key ingredient."

Susie Ings
Vahen's mother, mentor and dear friend

Our lives are meant to be lived out with *joy*! Yet events happen that can leave us feeling like we've been forgotten. What if you were told that even in the mess, the chaos, and yes, even in the self destruction, you were created to shine?

As the globe continues to navigate through a pandemic, Vahen gifts us with *Contagious Courage*. Vahen is a firecracker of a leader with a desperate heart to see our world encounter Jesus. Vahen tells stories penned with transparency and with you and I in mind. She unpacks scriptures that challenge us to face our insecurities, failures, and disappointments from a fresh perspective of *victory*. Her contagious spirit has ignited something within me and I'm positive it will leave its spark on you, too. You're not going to want to put this book down.

Jennilee Drisner
Owner & Photographer - Selah Reflections

Vahen King is the queen of courage. Diagnosed with a rare neurological disease, gutted by the loss of twins in a miscarriage, beset with relentless self-doubt, and a global pandemic that locked down opportunity, the former Miss Wheelchair Canada refused to lose! She trail-blazed her way forward with grit and grace. Vahen, as a friend and collaborator on events, has offered hope and promoted mental well-being.

Are you looking to face your fears and to know that you're enough and thus achieve your dreams? *Contagious Courage* will challenge you and show you how to create the right perspective to grow through what you go through. Vahen lays aside her armour on page one and shares personal experiences to show why trusting God and moving in obedience gives you access to more strength and courage than you ever thought possible. Vahen will inspire you with her vulnerability and humour to choose courage, embrace God's vision, and become unstoppable.

Rev. Bob Jones
Coach, blogger REVwords.com
Author: *You're Going To Be OK:*
Real Hope For Fighters of Cancer, Mental Illness, Sexual Abuse or Loss

If you want to know what courage looks like, Vahen is it. In this powerful book she takes you on a journey through grit and fire that has ignited her courage. Vahen had me at this statement, "What do we do with all this pain and suffering? I believe the bigger question is, "What can God do with all this pain and suffering." If you are ready to be ignited, then this book is a must read. You cannot read this book and not be filled with hope and faith. As I've learned from Vahen, courage is indeed contagious.

Connie Jakab
Owner - Brave Tribe
Author: *Culture Rebel - Because the world has enough desperate housewives*
Bring Them Closer - Calling parents to courage in the mental health crisis
When The Dead Live - Restoring ashes to beauty

Do any of you know someone that you are proud to say, "That's my friend!" Well, I felt that way while reading Vahen's story. I had heard about some of these experiences. I even witnessed a few as they were unfolding, but there was something fresh and powerful that I felt while sitting with this manuscript.

Contagious Courage is packed full of insightful truths and awe-inspiring moments that will leave the reader believing that freedom is possible! Vahen challenges us to "not waste our suffering" and teaches us that "you can never obey someone you don't trust or believe you are worthy of." This hit home for me. So often, many of us get caught in the "how" and get lost in the haze of our doubt and fear. It's human to want to control our pain and the outcome of our circumstances. Vahen highlights that it is only through surrender and trust that we are able to find true freedom.

Vahen's courage was forged in the fire, so expect to see these pages full of "fire statements." Her perseverance has produced a fruit which each of us get to taste and see that the Lord is good! It is evident to all who meet Vahen that she has a healed and joy-filled heart. That is the gift my friend brings to the world. So, Vahen, you did it! You WON TODAY!" And your love, joy, and courage is, in fact, contagious!

Adrienne Fudge
B.A. in Theology
Friend, Community Advocate, Missionary & Founder of Help the Help Inc.

Contagious Courage is one of the most inspiring books I have ever read. It's evident that Vahen shares her story of brokenness with a very unique purpose: to fill the hearts of other hurting individuals with a hope for a better tomorrow. That was my personal experience with reading *Contagious Courage*. I had found myself in one of the darkest periods of my life after experiencing an emotional breakdown and being hospitalized. I had reached a point where I had lost my will to live. Overwhelming sadness and despair were the only things I knew how to feel.

Then, through nothing short of a miracle, Vahen and I were connected through her brother. The next thing I knew Vahen offered me her book. God's timing was perfect. As I began reading this book I knew that I was indeed reading my survival guide! As a person who has experienced deep trauma, I felt that this book helped me start my own journey to finding hope and healing. The encouragement I received through Vahen's words filled my hurting heart with new hope for a better future. Reading *Contagious Courage* was the next step towards finding my purpose and will to live.

Danielle Broomfield
Friend

Life is filled with stories of challenges and celebrations. Vahen King, in her book, *Contagious Courage,* provides a glimpse of her struggles and victories in a candid and authentic way that will resonate with us all. She has navigated life with unique barriers and limitations which resulted in a journey of pain, brokenness, and ultimately breakthrough and transformation. The reader will vicariously experience the tenacity and grit with which she lived out her emotional, physical, and spiritual journey.

Vahen's faith-walk and love for God is contagious and is displayed in the many varied experiences of her life story to reach and maintain *living in freedom.* This book allows opportunity for the reader to journal as they read and reflect upon their own life with soul-searching questions.

I join with her in prayer that those giants that seem insurmountable in your life will fall and you , like Vahen, will move forward in total freedom from a courage that is truly transmissible. *Contagious Courage* will inspire and motivate you to pursue the heart of God. Enjoy this inspirational and encouraging read!

Pastor Terry W. Snow
General Superintendent
Pentecostal Assemblies of Newfoundland and Labrador

Vahen King has experienced an entire kaleidoscope of life experiences: blessing, challenges, failures, forgiveness, and Divine intervention and calling. From who she is and the life message that the Lord has given her, *Contagious Courage* is written. As she indicates, "It is my passion to see people overflowing with unexplainable peace! Defiant Joy! And contagious courage, so they can live in total freedom with unshakable faith and thriving in their God-given purpose." By recounting her own experiences and the life lessons she has learned and by incorporating the insights and experiences of others, Vahen provides a clear understanding how each of us can experience contagious courage.

Rev. David R. Wells M.A., D.D.
General Superintendent – The Pentecostal Assemblies of Canada
Surintendant Général - Les Assemblées de la Pentecôte du Canada
President – Pentecostal Charismatic Churches of North America
Author: *What I See* and *If Jesus*

The sign of a great book is always the author's ability to make you feel or emote as you read. That *is* the journey that is *Contagious Courage!* Vahen's story of trial and tribulation, a crazy health saga, highs and lows, joy and sadness... is one of the most emotional roller coasters that I have had the pleasure of reading!

Join Vahen on her incredible road to daily victories as you embark with her through stories that can only be described as the definition of courage. Her book is so aptly named as this incredible woman will literally make you want to know and experience *contagious courage*! You will ask yourself hard questions, shed a few tears, have a few "aha" moments, and (guaranteed) have a *proper* belly laugh. Vahen's courage *is* contagious and her heart is grace-filled. I urge you to pick up this book, prepare yourself with maybe a few tissues just in case, and enjoy the experience that is *Contagious Courage!*

Ethan Nicolas
Owner: PityTheFool Fitness
Author: *Grit To Grace* (coming soon)

Vahen is a communicator of courage by her very life! Sadly, in our world, negativity, fear, and anxiety are spreading at epidemic proportions. In contrast, Vahen's latest book will challenge you to break out of your comfort zone where you'll catch her contagious courage spirit and live a braver, bolder life! She'll guide you throughout the pages, making *you* a transmitter for contagious courage!

Sherry Stahl
Speaker, Bible Teacher, Founder of The Soul H20 Blog, Radio Host
Author: *Water in the Dessert, Soul H2O*

In Contagious Courage, Vahen remarks: "Facing your fears and conquering them changes your self-perception." After reading her recent book, I have been greatly impacted by her spirit of courage and resilience. Her openness and honesty are totally refreshing and the life applications she shares are transforming. Treat yourself to a journey of growth and hope as you encounter a passionate heart of faith and joy.

Rev. Ronald Rust
Lead Pastor-Trinity Pentecostal Church ,Montreal
International Speaker and Bible College Educator

It is amazing how people find courage in the midst of tragedy and are then able to overcome the odds! That is the story of Vahen King who has not just survived what appeared to be insurmountable odds but has thrived. She now is sharing in this book *Contagious Courage* the secrets to overcoming the odds in a practical and engaging way. You will find in these pages the raw courage she discovered within and the lessons learned that can help you overcome whatever you are facing. I highly recommend *Contagious Courage*. I know that time spent reading and applying the lessons learned will change your life!

Larry M Scarbeau
Overcomer Coach

This book is like no others. It is more than just reading words on a page—it is a conversation. Vahen King courageously opens up her heart and soul to you to share her triumphs and heartaches. But then, also asks you questions that you are compelled to answer.

Vahen's words are raw and real. The fear and uncertainty that has been caused by isolation during the pandemic reinforces just how essential connection with others is. Every day waking up questioning who we are, why we're here, and what's coming next can mark our days. Vahen helps to show you that you are NOT alone, even when it feels like it. We are going to need all the courage we can get in this new world.

Vahen's life stories are examples of how to rise above difficult times and to find joy in the most difficult moments of your life. She challenges you to let someone love you even when you feel broken. Can you do it? The words in this book, *Contagious Courage*, are the tools your emotional survival guide shouldn't be without.

Tracie Gray
Television Reporter, Radio Announcer
Actor, Writer & Comedian

There is certainly no value to pain for pain's own sake. But suffering correlated to the Creator's promise to transform it into hope is highlighted in Vahen's story. Her journey through the hard times as presented in Contagious Courage, is proof that God can use adversity to teach us what we would never have discovered by pursuing the illusion of a stress-free life.

Gary Taitinger
Superintendent of PAOC AB&NWT District

Foreword

I have known Vahen for all of her life. She is my sister. Growing up with her was interesting, to say the least. I have witnessed firsthand her emotional ups and down, poor decision-making and yes, her desperate desire to be the center of attention. Actually, being quite honest, if I base my opinion on our early years, I would doubt her ability to be a leader, motivator or inspirational speaker. There was no middle ground with Vahen. Things were always very good or very bad, and she wanted everyone around her to know why. I could definitely tell stories of "little-sister escapades" and "big-brother rescue attempts."

So, my sister wrote a book... WHAT! She wrote it and published it and it's been changing lives ever since...mine included. I have to say that I am so proud of Vahen's work, including her first book entitled *Going Farther*. I heard a long time ago that God can take our garbage and turn it into a treasure. Vahen's willingness to be transparent and share the worst parts of her life for God's glory shows that we do not have to let the past dictate our future. This is what my sister did in her first book and continues to do it here through the pages of Contagious Courage! Her readiness to be vulnerable as well as her contagious courage is indeed changing lives. I have seen firsthand how Vahen's passion to ignite hearts with hope is God's hand extended.

From my experience working in the area of mental health and addictions, I have come to know that people want to have someone hear their story and care about them. So, when Vahen came to speak at my workplace, it was simply remarkable to see how her story ignited hope in this seemingly hopeless environment. One staff member at the hospital even said, "Vahen, what you did by coming here was nothing short of amazing." She continued, "No one comes here! No one comes to share hope or inspiration. So by coming here today, doing what you did, you have no idea how much that was noticed and received." Another co-worker shared "Mrs. King was able to capture the attention of our youth experiencing addiction and mental health concerns in a matter of seconds. Her ability to build rapport was evident from the moment she spoke. She started by making us laugh. She provided a safe and open space in a room with a very vulnerable population. She was down-to-earth, funny, and a champion for wellness in mental health."

Contagious Courage will indeed ignite hope in the hearts of its readers. Vahen has a refreshing ability to be real and reach people where they are. Her story is relatable. Pain is something we have all experienced. The tragic experiences that she's had to live through, however, have given her the credentials to speak in many settings and to help many come to the amazing revelation that there is hope.

As Vahen's brother and friend, I love that God is using her story for His glory. She has allowed God to do His work. As she conveys from her own life about the process of recycling pain, others will be helped along in their journey. God's love is spread throughout the pages of my sister's story in ways I never thought possible. It is proof that hope shines the brightest in the darkest places. I believe that her positive message is a powerful tool that will help people truly find healing, freedom, and contagious courage. As a co-worker said for both of us, "Her first book is on my office shelf as inspiration and I will be placing her second one there, too."

Carl Ings, BRec, CTRS
Recreation Development Specialist

Introduction

How many of you ever set out to do something, yet were consumed by fear, and felt totally unqualified? "Most people who are known for being courageous have one thing in common – they don't describe themselves as courageous. They talk about being afraid and scared."[1] Well that's this girl. I understand those words, more than you know!

Did I really think that I could write a book titled 'Going Farther' and expect that I could just sit back? I just reached one destination with God only to see that He wants to take me even farther.

Going farther or receiving more sounds very exciting, doesn't it? Well, it is. I have seen God do tremendous things in my life. I am experiencing more blessing than I ever hoped or dreamed of. But, if I am honest, I'll tell you that I have said to God more than once: "Can't you see how hard I'm working?" "I don't have any more to give." "Can't you do the rest?" "I'm done."

Have you ever watched that show, "The Biggest Loser?" You see people getting pushed to their breaking point, yelling at their trainers, and wanting to quit because they thought they would physically break under the intense pressure. Yet the final show would always reveal the incredible results. And the "biggest loser" would be singing a different tune as you see them often in tears thanking their trainer for pushing them. Just like that 'biggest loser' who saw their desired weight loss, I also had a change in perspective when I saw growth in my spiritual life. Once I got over my frustration and accepted the discomfort of the growing process, I was able to be excited and thank God for giving me the courage to push through and grow stronger. This process really revealed the frailty of my own strength and allowed me to access more of His. At times it was truly terrifying to trust in *His* process and training.

Change *is* hard work whether it's physical, mental or spiritual, and it requires all your courage. It forces you to ditch your "I can't" mentality and

---

1 Rev. Bob Jones, *4 Ironic Characteristics of the Courageous*
https://revwords.com/4-characteristics-of-courage/ (Online 2021, January)

lean into discomfort. Scary? Yes, but you *can* do it and it's *so* worth it!

Many of you may already know my story but allow me to introduce myself to those who may not yet know me. My name is Vahen King. On May 30, 1999, I contracted a virus called transverse myelitis that left me partially paralyzed and confined to a wheelchair. This all happened *one* week after receiving an engagement ring from the love of my life. It`s the love story about my knight in shining armour (as I refer to him) and how he chose to stay with this girl who was told she may never walk again. Walking down the aisle on May 13, 2000 with my parents on my wedding day, I was not only fulfilling my dreams, but I was beating the odds.

I'd like to make a bold statement and say, "Every giant you face is an opportunity for an even *bigger* victory." A life-altering disability, my infidelity, and feeling trapped as a prisoner of fear were only a few of my giants. What giants would you like to see fall in your life? It could be giants of fear, rejection, anger, pride, or need for control. Your list could be short or long. Take a moment to consider any giants standing in your path.

It is only in the "looking back" that I can recognize the key elements that became part of the bigger victory. With each new battle came the realization that the biggest limitations or disabilities were often the ones I put on myself. I still face new giants – they don't go away; but it gets easier to overcome them, knowing I'm not doing it alone or in my own strength.

I continue to think of myself as a courageous giant slayer in training! My "pain journey" led me to find more blessings than I could have ever hoped for or imagined. I have unshakable faith, unexplainable peace, defiant joy, and contagious courage.

In 2017 I was crowned the first-ever Miss Wheelchair Canada. I went on to win the prestigious title of Miss Kindness World at the Miss Wheelchair World pageant in Warsaw, Poland.

I am an author, speaker, and founder of the non-profit charity which I've appropriately titled *"Going Farther."* I am now living with my prince charming, Vaughan, in Edmonton, Alberta. I have traveled nationally and internationally sharing my story of hope and courage in churches, schools, and community events. And, all this is happening from my wheelchair with the support of people like him and you. If you ask anyone who knows me, they'll agree I'm just a confidently imperfect girl who said yes to God with a willingness to seize every opportunity to inspire and empower others to *go farther and access their own contagious courage.*

You will often hear me say, "You can't control what happens to you, but you can control how you respond." I want to acknowledge that when my life was turned upside down by a paralyzing virus, that was definitely outside of my control. In contrast, the challenges (or giants as I sometimes call them in this book) I faced as a result of my poor life choices were *not* out of my control. I made those choices, so what now? Would I remain "stuck" in a destructive spiral or choose to make positive choices and begin moving forward?

In my first book, *Going Farther,* I tell you of a journey I would not have chosen to take. Yet, that journey shows the beauty of what God can do with our pain and brokenness when surrendered to Him. People may see a happy marriage, a crown, and my titles, but not understand the giants I've had to battle.

Since becoming a person with a disability, I have experienced more barriers and limitations emotionally, physically and spiritually than ever before. Yet, I have never been more free. Through that intense process Jesus became my personal friend whom I trust with my life. And as a result, I have learned obedience, faith, and discipline. These are three words I want you to get used to seeing. They are key elements which have helped me discover and maintain my freedom and contagious courage.

God keeps reminding me that if I am not moving forward, I will eventually go backwards. He was developing in me a level of courage I didn't know existed. Or if it did exist, I didn't think it was for me. Do you know that same courage exists for you, too? I know I could never have discovered and experienced this courage to go farther or receive more without my faith and the discipline to work at it daily.

No matter where you are in your journey of freedom and courage, I want you to feel as if I am sitting with you at your kitchen table (or wherever you usually visit in your home) and having a personal conversation. As I share my experiences of giants I've fought and the process I've walked to reach and maintain my freedom, I want you to hear my heart.

I will be asking questions along the way as if in conversation. At times, I'll even refer to a chart or a diagram that I have included in the chapter or at the back of my book to help you benefit even more from our time together. And if you choose to journal (which is not required, but highly recommended), I would actually love to hear from you so I can hear your side of this conversation. I will envision sitting with you, sipping my hot tea, and sharing these growing experiences together.

Morgan Harper Nichols said, "Tell the story of the mountain you climbed. Your words could be a page in someone else's survival guide."[2] If you notice my book title, it also includes the word *contagious*. That is because when I discovered that *my* courage had the power to unlock other people's freedom, it was a whole new way to live. I want to provide you with some tools that I hope will be a part of *your* survival guide and help you take that first step or the *next step to* keep moving forward.

It is my prayer that you see those giants in your life fall and that you, too, move forward in total freedom with a courage that is contagious. Before you head into battle, may I suggest my "Battle Cry" prayer as additional words for your survival guide. Are you ready?

My Battle Cry

Fear, you don't own me!
I am approved by Christ and declare that I have full freedom and
confidence in Him.
This is my battle cry.

You wanted to limit me with my pain and brokenness, yet I found
Someone who makes me limitless in spite of my cracks.
I have the Champion of all champions who is on my side.

---

2 Morgan Harper Nichols, Instagram quote, https://www.instagram.com/p/Bi96Mb1hnXZ/?hl=en/ (Online 2021, January)

He tells me I am a warrior! A fighter!
This is my battle cry.

I have authority over all the powers that threaten to destroy me.
All fear, condemnation, self-pity, unbelief, unforgiveness, and
unworthiness have no right to take up space in my mind. I am
renewed by the Word of God.
This is my battle cry.

Yes, there are times I am tempted to fear, but I am not a slave to it.
I chose to walk by faith and not by what I see or feel!
This is my battle cry.

I AM forgiven!
I AM worthy!
I AM confident in who I am in Christ!
I AM loved.
The pressure from my attacker only produces more power in me.
This is my battle cry!

I am an overcomer by the power of Jesus in me.
I turn pain into power.
I see opposition as opportunities.
I will arise and shine because it is Christ who gives me the courage
to obey and the strength to fight.
This is my battle cry.

Contagious courage and strength are my inheritance!
With all my armour on, I'm ready to fight!
Nothing can puncture my spirit.
Because I'm better under pressure.
This is my battle cry.

My heart is ignited with hope, I have undeniable peace, defiant joy,
and contagious courage!
This is my battle cry.

Section I

Courage Is Possible!

Strength to Fight

I see the flames of life dance before my eyes
Remind me that you're here once again
I see the sands of time as they cloud my mind
Remind me that you're here once again

I'm sinking in the silence, there's a battle deep inside
It's hard to keep believing when I've lost my reason why

You give me the strength to fight, push aside my pride
My fears won't conquer me
You give me the strength to fight, I have drawn the line
I know you're here with me

With no end in sight and no strength to rise
Remind me that you're here once again
I'm sinking in the silence, there's a battle deep inside
It's hard to keep believing when I've lost my reason why

You give me the strength to fight, push aside my pride
My fears won't conquer me
You give me the strength to fight, I have drawn the line
I know you're here with me

You give me the strength to fight, I have drawn the line
I know you're here with me[1]

---

1 Strength to Fight, Tamara Boyes, CD Baby; CD Baby Pro Publishing (2019)

Where to Begin When You're Building Again

"God gave you to me." "I want to work on us." Hearing these words for the first time from a hospital bed after just being told that I'd never walk again was the most incredible thing. However, I never imagined hearing "I want to work on us" with the additional "I forgive you" after my betrayal and infidelity.

Vaughan and I did rebuild our lives again. We managed to stumble forward and ultimately get through it. However, in order to navigate through that painful "rebuilding" process, we had to allow the Lord to *move in* and *work in* both our hearts. And, we had to *apply* the grace available to us so we could experience the "more" He had always intended for our lives.

Yes, it was great hearing those words which now included "I forgive you." And you would *think* it would have been enough to help me feel love or give me the courage to be free. Right? Unfortunately, it was quite the opposite. I was overwhelmed even more. You see, it was easier for me to walk away than to stay and face my husband. I had been unfaithful. I had lived a secret life of deception and lies. I had hurt myself and those around me! How could Vaughan ever *really* love and trust me again? Fear, guilt, and shame were the walls of the prison surrounding me and severing any connection to my husband. In *my* mind, I was not worthy of true love or happiness. I didn't feel very courageous; and I was definitely not free.

To give you a vivid picture of where I was and how difficult that season was for me, I'll ask you this: "Have you ever watched someone trying to rescue a seal caught in a net?"

The seal is all tangled up in that net, yet it wants to be free. It doesn't know that the intention of the rescuer is to free it. The seal fights back, resisting the one trying to rescue it. The net becomes bound around the seal so tightly that its skin gets cut and actually starts bleeding. But it continues to resist the one trying to help. The rescuer could even suffer a bite or two from the seal.

Well, that was me. I was wounded, hurt, and confused by all the trauma. I didn't know how to get help or understand what my real needs were. I resisted the people closest to me who were trying to help. I especially resisted Vaughan and hurt him deeply. Yet, he saw through my pain and hung on to me until I was able to see that I *was* worth loving. It was because Vaughan and those closest to me chose to fight and not give up on me that I was ultimately able to see I could be free of these things that had me all tangled up.

Don't get me wrong. It was great to receive that love and forgiveness and I truly wanted to change, but *could* I change? I didn't even know where to start!

If there could be road signs on life's journey, I would definitely want you to see a flashing yellow caution light as you take this next step with me. Just ahead on the pathway is *letting go* to walk by faith. Letting go is scary, because it's terrifying to step out into the unknown. I was more acquainted with the pain than with the faith and courage change required of me. And from where I was sitting, I was actually more comfortable with my pain than with the discomfort of change.

Loving me without judgment, was the only way Vaughan was able to love me where I was. Were there tough conversations? Yes! Were there arguments and hurt feelings? Absolutely! But not once did Vaughan make me feel guilty or call me a bad name in the heat of any of those times. I will always be grateful that God's grace allowed him to embrace *me* and the process. Then the impossible became possible and we began to see measurable growth.

Blockages To Rebuilding

Whenever we embark upon a path of change, we quickly become very aware that there are blockages within us. We may not be able to accurately name these blockages or know how to remove them at the time. Yet, they all are contributing factors to our lived reality.

Since contracting the virus, part of my "new normal" with my physical disability was that things took so much more time and effort. I was constantly struggling with my level of physical energy and I didn't know why. I was tired *all* the time and found it *really* hard to focus. But I thought that maybe it was a symptom of what I had to live with as a person with a disability. And the inability to focus or comprehend? I thought that was because I wasn't very smart and I would just have to accept that I couldn't understand like other people. I was living every day feeling like *everyone else* was better and smarter than me. Talk about having something shoot your confidence or self esteem!

That whole time I didn't even realize that I had a hypo-thyroid condition. My doctor explained it to me like this: "It's like you have a 4-cylinder engine, but it's only running on one! And that inability for your body to keep up with you is affecting your ability to focus, etc." I was like, "Yes! That's exactly how I feel!"

The doctor said that it would take a while for me to feel the effects of the medication he prescribed. But actually, the results I *felt* were immediate! For the first time in a long time I *understood* what was happening with me and knew there was a solution. Emotionally, that lifted something off me that I couldn't explain. After a few weeks I regained my ability to focus. That gave me more confidence and I felt more equipped to handle life. I was like a new woman.

While we don't all have known or unknown medical conditions, you may relate to being tired and running on empty. You may experience limited ability to handle stress and conflict to your full capacity. When you are going through life just reacting to the things it throws at you, you begin to walk around defeated with low confidence.

You're not really free nor do you realize there are things that you can access that will help you. If that's you, I would like to say that seeking medical help for your mental or physical health is vital.

My undetected medical condition was limiting my ability to see clearly and function or react in a healthy way to the challenges I was facing. I was exerting *so* much energy but seeing no results and getting even more frustrated.

If I didn't even know there was a problem, how was I going to resolve it? Am I the only one who's been blindsided this way? "The most dangerous place in the world is *not* standing in a minefield, rather the most dangerous place in the world is standing in a minefield that you didn't know was there."[1]

The same principle applied to the changes I needed to make in my broken relationships. You see, no matter how many times I was told "I love you" and "You are forgiven," for my mistakes. I didn't even realize that I also had to love and forgive myself. And when you don't realize that *you're the problem*, that's a problem! The only way I was able to get back up was with God's help. I had to accept God's love and forgiveness. I had to learn to forgive myself and stop blaming others for my mistakes. That was hard; but that was only the *beginning* of my long road back. Forgiveness is a truly remarkable thing when you experience it, but I had to also believe that, with God's help, it *was* possible to become free and *stay* free.

What if I had blocked my freedom by continuing to hang onto my pain, pride, fears, or need for control? It would be just like what I would continue to experience if I hadn't taken the medication I needed. I would still have been only going through the motions, dragging myself along, and not having the energy to cope with life's challenges. As I began to surrender to the Lord, I started experiencing more freedom. I was now finally regarding myself worthy of His love. I began to desire more of Him. I *needed* more! The future of our marriage (and our destiny) depended on it.

1　Unknown

Before we get to those dynamic steps of surrender, we can continue to learn about "building again" by reviewing some of the other blockages we discovered and overcame.

There were multiple factors complicating that season of our lives. These losses became challenging blockages. One major factor was the miscarriage we had during the time we were trying to rebuild our marriage. (We will open our hearts and share in detail in the next chapter about our losses surrounding the miscarriage and the grace of God to rebuild, but for now I want to stay on the blockages and things that hold us back.)

Filling the Void of the Loss

Whenever there is a loss, there is a potential blockage that can come from how we choose to fill the void that is left. This became the major climate of my betrayal and infidelity. I had this chasm-sized hole in my heart and I had no idea how I would fill it. That chasm formed what seemed to be an unbridgeable gap between Vaughan and I. Oh, the pain that resulted from that faulty conclusion. When you are in emotional pain, you resort to desperate measures to *numb* the pain. We both contributed to the drift apart. Vaughan had become immersed in on-line video games and seemed to be emotionally checked out. I started making bigger compromises. I started lying to Vaughan about where I was and who I was with. But was this a life I really wanted? No! You might be thinking, "Well, you chose it!" Yes, I did, but I was a very unhappy person desperately trying to fill that void! Inside I was drifting away and Vaughan didn't seem to notice or care.

I remember the day I made up my mind to leave Vaughan and move out. I was done! That was my decision, not because I felt it was *best,* but I just knew *I wasn't happy. I was desperate for solutions but had none. I felt trapped and lost.* I wasn't that same loving, soft-hearted girl he fell in love with. I was just pretending and I knew he deserved better.

I asked a friend who was also struggling with her relationship if she would get a place with me. When she said, "Sorry, I can't," then I spent the next week trying to find a place (an accessible place) that I could afford on my own. And believe it or not, I even asked God to help me find a place! No luck. But in the days that followed, Vaughan and I had the first glimpse of a breakthrough. I confessed everything to him and told him about my affair, and that our marriage was over, expecting to have him leave.

As you would expect, my announcement totally shocked and stunned Vaughan. He left our apartment to stay with his family while he tried to sort through my betrayal. After several days we got together again and spent hours talking everything out in a neutral place. We agreed poor choices had been made by both of us. He chose to stay and start over again *if* I was willing to do the same. I didn't understand how this would work, but I was willing to try. I didn't have much hope, but I was willing to be honest. Vaughan hung onto me and fought for me.

The very next day after I decided to stay in our marriage, my friend said, "OK, I'm ready to leave, I'll move in with you." In *that* moment I knew it was God protecting me when I wasn't able to protect myself. And while I was simply going through the motions of staying to attempt to work on my marriage, I *was,* at least willing to try. Even in my pain I started to thank God. While it was only a faint whimpering, I was thankful even though I was almost resenting Him for the closed door to leave. Deep down I knew it was Him. And while I felt alone, I most definitely was not. I need to say here that when God rebuilds, He doesn't do things the way we want or in our time. He does it better!

If you are taking notes or if you want to remember anything that I say in *Contagious Courage*, don't miss this: it's common for people experiencing trauma to block things out. They do not think clearly nor are they able to make sound decisions. But until you experience it, you can't truly understand it. So, loving them where they are without judgment is *huge*.

I had to lean often into Vaughan's confidence that we could heal and that change *was* possible. I had even told him at one point that my level of confidence could be compared to my ability to remove the freckles from my arm!

Yet, I didn't want to live in that kind of *fear of failure* every day. It seemed like an impossible challenge. Somehow, despite all my fears, I meant it when I said "I'll try."

So, when I tell you that the process of rebuilding *me* and my marriage did not happen overnight, I know you believe me. I had to heal before I could have a healthy marriage. Little by little we discovered and dealt with the unresolved issues that had chipped away at our relationship.

Change Breaks the Chains

We made some big changes. I quit my job and distanced myself from my old lifestyle and influences. We rebuilt our social environment and re-prioritized our lives and goals. And we implemented practical ways to build trust and mutual accountability.

One of the biggest "practical" and most powerful things we did to rebuild was having full access to each other's emails, passwords, and social medial accounts. I can almost hear the gasp as you read that. I recall the response I received when I asked this question at a couples' retreat. I said, "I wonder if I were to ask you to give your phones to your spouse or significant other right now without erasing any history, would you be willing? And if you did, what would they find?" Well, you could have heard a pin drop. Maybe you think that is excessive? Whether you're married or not, let me ask you this: "Are there "secret things" that you are afraid to share that are affecting your ability to have a deeper relationship with God or those close to you?"

In our rebuilding, another important step for us was to have a fresh start. That's when we decided to pack up and move to Edmonton. When all we had was each other, we truly were able to start building again. I can be honest here and tell you that I hadn't fallen back in love with Vaughan yet. Some days I felt like he was breathing for both of us and that was enough to keep us alive. For way too long I wondered if I would ever be happy again—let alone be free or have courage. After what we had just been through, I didn't think it was possible. But we were *still together* and that was *something.* You may have heard me say, my story is about so much more than "he stayed." By now, I'm sure you're catching a glimpse of that truth.

Another important element in the rebuilding process was the power of praying parents. Talk about someone not giving up on you when you didn't want help. There wasn't *one* phone call that didn't end with, "I love you and we are praying for you." I know my mom could write her *own* book, but let's just say that sometimes those phrases would literally cause me to get angry and at times hang up on them—even though those prayers may very well have been what saved my life. For that, I am so grateful. I can't thank them enough for "praying through to completion."

Looking back, I now realize that in order to slay the giants of fear and intimidation and find the courage to walk in freedom, that first step toward healing was to *receive* love even when I didn't feel worthy. I want to celebrate it again: it was Vaughan's love and the love of those close to me that helped me understand and truly feel God's unconditional love. Vaughan was willing to love me where I was at, just like *God* was willing to love me where I was at. That unconditional love began to dissolve the notion that I wasn't good enough to be loved.

Trusting "The Builder"

I couldn't see how it was possible, but I had to ⌐ ⌐ ⌐ strength and learn to trust again. However, how can we love if we don't trust the person we are following? Good question. That is what made those initial steps so terrifying yet so important if we were going to rebuild. Yes, I was forgiven, but I had not yet learned to completely let go and trust. But I was willing to try. I had to fall in love with *both* God and Vaughan all over again. I had to trust that they would never let me down, even though for the longest time I believed that they both had.

Looking back, I now understand that each lie I had believed over the years about myself and God led me to lower my shield of faith. Those lies were like arrows to my heart and became the "unknown blockages" that started to re-define my view of God. That's when I began losing my trust in God and making little compromises. I really don't believe people realize just how *harmful* these little compromises are. Kay Arthur said, "Sin takes you farther than you ever expected to go; keeps you longer than you ever intended to stay, and costs more than you ever expected to pay."[2] Infidelity! Loss of identity! I paid a high price indeed.

Eventually, I lost my personal relationship with God and as a result I lost the ability to discern His voice or trust the God I had always loved. I had known the freedom of simple childlike faith. In that kind of faith, I knew God loved me. And if I made a mistake, I would ask forgiveness and He would forgive. There was no shame attached to that. And spoiler alert: God used Vaughan to be the true example of that unconditional love I had craved. You'll often hear me say, "Vaughan was Jesus with skin on." However, let me just say, that while God will use people to be His hands and feet, no one can fill the longing of your heart except Him. We'll come back to this.

We sometimes make bad choices in our pain; and those bad choices often lead us down a path we feel we can't find our way back

---

2 Kay Arthur, https://www.allchristianquotes.org/quotes/Kay_Arthur/2402/ (Online 2021, January)

om. Though that may be true, I have also learned the flip side of that. Each small choice I made in obedience to God took me one step closer to my freedom. Through this painful process, the Lord was faithful to weave love, joy, peace and courage into this warrior's wounded heart.

No matter where I am in my journey, there are three things that help me *maintain* my freedom and courage. These three are essential: being obedient to *His* voice, getting really good at waiting (faith), and the discipline to keep in step with the Lord.

Where are you in your journey? Are you feeling overwhelmed today? Maybe you are trapped in a situation that is causing you to lose hope? Maybe trapped in a secret addiction that you want out of? Maybe you are consumed with shame or guilt and you wonder if anyone can love you? I challenge you to be transparent, give up control, and let someone love you in your brokenness. But more than that, learn to love yourself. Perhaps letting God love you right where you are is your first *big* step. Maybe you're not ready yet. That's okay; He's a gentleman and will wait with you and for you! If you're reading this and you have healthy relationships, or you just want to go farther and have *even more* freedom, I'll have more for you later. But I will ask you this: Is there someone close to you who needs you to love them *where they are? Without judgment?*

As I reflect on Vaughan and me as "that couple who almost didn't make it," I can honestly say that if sharing our story helps just one person find the courage to get up or rebuild again, it *is* worth it. With confidence I can declare this scripture to be true in my life in ways I never had before: *"My grace is sufficient for you, for my power is made perfect in weakness. Therefore, I will boast all the more gladly about my weaknesses, so that Christ's power may rest on me." 2 Corinthians 12:9 (NIV)*

Chapter 2

CTRL-Z

I remember when I transitioned from using a typewriter to typing on a computer for the first time. I couldn't believe it: I went from the frustration of waiting for the liquid white-out to dry before retyping over my mistakes to the luxury of saving and editing *right there* on the *same* document!

Life changing. But nothing brought more excitement to my essay writing than the day I was told about CTRL-Z. I was like, let me get this straight: You mean all I have to do is keep pressing CTRL-Z to undo my mistakes and start over? For those of you who are laughing at me because I'm dating myself, or if you don't know what a typewriter is, it's okay. Undoubtedly, all of us can relate to the world of technology and how it has indeed been life-changing.

But, why am I talking to you about CTRL-Z? Well, I wonder, how many of us have wished we could do that with a text message or an email we've sent or with words spoken? What about that season of your life or that relationship for which you wish you could have a "do over?" James R. Sherman says, "Though no one can go back and make a brand-new start, anyone can start from now and make a brand-new ending."[1]

I can tell you from the story of our lives that a "do-over" is possible but it's not instant. There really are no CTRL-Z keys to push as we're living our lives. But change *is* possible. The Lord has committed Himself to us, to walking with us through the darkest parts of our story. He's our Redeemer and He can make all things beautiful "in spite of" the dark and ugly of our lives. For Vaughan and I, this truth is a lived reality. Yes, we experienced the life-altering transverse myelitis which attacked my body just after we were engaged. But part of our story includes the miscarriage during the time we

---

1   James R. Sherman, *Rejection*, (Published by Pathway Books, Golden Valley, Minnesota. 1982), 35.

were rebuilding our lives. That loss, compounded because of the doctor's conclusion that we were pregnant with twins, definitely became a major life-shaping element in our CTRL-Z story.

How could two little ones we never had a chance to meet be used so extensively in *our* "do over"? But, that's exactly what our gracious Heavenly Father did.

Let me take you back to the night we lost these two little ones. And as I walk you through the events that followed, you'll be able to see the hand of God. You'll see how He takes those dark and ugly parts of our lives that threaten to keep us stuck and turns them into something beautiful that can heal us.

On the night that I miscarried, Vaughan was due to leave on a business trip early the next morning. I remember feeling numb with shock and grief, but he seemed oblivious to what had just happened. He continued with his plans and left a few hours later. Even though I hadn't asked him to stay, I felt abandoned when he headed out the door to the airport. I could not begin to embrace the depth of my loss.

That next morning when I woke up alone, I was just a lifeless body. I was numb to any real emotion. I called my sister and told her I lost the babies. Her immediate response was, "I'm coming." The next day my sister was by my side and insisted that I take time off work. I am thankful that she was there for me, facilitating the arrangements at a time when I didn't know what I needed or wanted.

That same week my mother-in- law called offering to take me to my "DNC" appointment. I might not remember much about the details of that appointment, but one thing that screams from the memory of that day was how emotional I got when I realized I could *not* have done this alone. And while my mother-in-law insisted that she didn't feel as if she had done much, I couldn't thank her enough. I have told her many times: "Mom King, just you *being* there *was* exactly what I needed in a time when I felt abandoned."

About a year or so after the miscarriage, I showed my sister a few things I had purchased while I was pregnant. She said, "Vahen, this is the first time you have ever talked about the pregnancy or the details surrounding the miscarriage. I didn't even know the doctor had told you that it looked like you miscarried twins! It's nice to finally hear you talk about it."

When it was time to write about this traumatic event in my first book *Going Farther,* I actually had to talk to my sister to help me recall an accurate picture. My entire recollection of this time was foggy at best. When we started discussing more details of the miscarriage, she helped me uncover things I didn't even remember.

I was shocked when she told me that I had seemed to be minimizing the entire loss. As she listened to me, she realized I had never appropriately *grieved* that painful loss. I later learned that this response is quite typical of denial. I would also come to understand that denial can become a *pattern of response.* (Stay tuned for our very unexpected discovery of some of the beginnings of my well-established *pattern* of denial. Spoiler alert, it will be related to how we omitted the huge step of grieving the losses brought about by the virus that attacked my body leaving me in this wheelchair.)

You may remember the analogy of the seal caught in the net. This was another example of me wanting to be free, but not knowing how. In the hours after the miscarriage denial was so apparent, but not to me! I had really needed my sister to help me even figure out what to do next, but I didn't even know to ask. She said, "Vahen, when I suggested that you take a little time off work, your initial response was that you didn't think it was necessary. That's when I knew that everything was locked up inside, and I knew I had to help you."

That's the thing with denial: you don't know you're doing it! But, acknowledging the denial and getting in touch with our painful realities that we "stuff away" might just be the beautifully ugly part of the process that helps us get to the next stage of healing.

About 3 years after our miscarriage, Vaughan and I received the tragic news of a dear friend and her husband who just had a miscarriage. I remember Vaughan saying that was so sad. He continued to talk about it with such compassion. As I sat there, I was in a little disbelief. I mean, I know it's sad, but I had this moment where I stopped and looked at him and, without sounding accusatory, said, "Yes it is, and you know, Vaughan, that's exactly what I went through."

My husband is not an emotional guy who cries easily, but he spontaneously reached over and held me with tears in his eyes and said, "*I'm so sorry I left you that morning.*" That totally unexpected response was followed by, "Tell me about that day; I want to know." As I shared, I couldn't believe what happened next. When I got to the part where the doctor had said it was twins, he once again leaned over and embraced me and said. "I would have wanted twins! I am *so* sorry." Let's just say that there was *more* healing available to us both that day that made our love grow even stronger.

Let's fast forward to January 19, 2018, 15 years after the miscarriage. I was telling Vaughan about an event that I spoke at and how I met this young girl named Jael. I told him that she reminded me of my childhood faith. Through meeting her, God showed me I *do* have that child like faith again. As I was sharing this with Vaughan he asked, "What did you say her name was?" Well, you will not believe what he said next. He told me that back when we were "expecting" he daydreamed a little about names we would use if we had a boy or girl. He continued to say that he had "Jael" as one of the girl names on his short list. I said (kinda laughing and a little in disbelief), "What??, and when were you going to share this with me?" But, in all honesty, as time went on, I guess it just hadn't really mattered. But the story doesn't stop there.

January 26, 2018, one week after this conversation, I was at the ONE CONFERENCE in Edmonton. I was listening to a presentation from Compassion Canada. While I definitely felt a tug in my heart, I didn't know if it was because I was to sponsor a child or just that I was simply so moved by the touching story.

Well, as I attempted to continue my day and go to my next lecture, I couldn't shake the feeling that I needed to go and see if the Compassion Canada booth had a girl named Jael! I actually thought it was a way to get off the hook. That's not a very common name, so I kind of said, "*Okay, God. If there's a Jael, I'll sponsor her.*" I went to the booth and told them the same story I've just told you about Vaughan, etc. The lady at the Compassion Canada booth, now in tears, gushed, "That's a beautiful story!" But as she glanced down at all the boxes of children's donor cards she continued, "Nothing here is in alphabetical order, so to find a specific name would be almost impossible. Also, in all of my years working with Compassion Canada, I have never seen that name. Many a Carlos, but never a Jael."

By this time the manager was also enthralled with my story and added, "Let me take your name and number and tonight I'll look in the database to see if I can find a match." As he was writing down my contact information another of the staff shouts, "I found it!" He responded and said, "You found what?" She said, "I found a Jael." Now we are all in tears and I can't believe my eyes and ears. She continued, "But it's a girl; is that okay?" I said, "Yep, it's supposed to be." Then, she finished with a remark that left our jaws on the floor! She said, in a sad voice, "But, she's 15!" (She had assumed I wanted a toddler because, typically, everyone looks for the young cute kids.) That just pushed me into a full-on ugly cry! Immediately, I knew I had to sponsor Jael. Do the math! She would have been born just about the time our twins were due! I couldn't wait any longer. Without hesitation, I was signing on the dotted line and being interviewed by Compassion Canada. They felt this was a story that needed to be shared. Let's back up one moment. The instant I heard they found Jael and knew I had to sponsor her, my response was "I can't have this baby without Vaughan being on board." And we all laughed! By now I'm sure you'll all agree: When God heals or does a "CTRL-Z", He does it with amazing detail!

Forgiveness Set Me Free

My life experiences have given me a crash course in understanding the *process* of creating that "do over," but also on forgiveness—one that I certainly did not pass with flying colours.

And now that you know more of our story, let me share the faulty view I held so long about forgiveness. I feel that exposing and shedding the faulty thinking can be another key element in that process which helps us move forward. I confess that forgiveness for me was like a four-letter word.

At times it reminded me of what I felt unworthy of. Other times I used it inappropriately and threw the word around without much thought. Let's just say my words didn't match my heart. But the truth is, the topic of forgiveness made me very uncomfortable.

As an adult, I loved the Lord but was quite content to keep a (faulty!) mindset that, "God will forgive me so I don't really need to give up x, y, or z." Nor do I really need to forgive "that" person. My tainted view was: "No one is perfect, so I can do whatever I want (even hold on to a *little* unforgiveness) and God will still love me, right?" And while it is true that God doesn't withdraw His love from us, I will tell you that it is no way to live.

I am so thankful that I came to the point that I no longer wanted to live a life where I was just "getting by." I wanted *more*. I hated living in fear and being tossed around and taken down by every challenge that came. I no longer wanted to be controlled by my emotions and seemingly by the people in my circumstances. I guess hanging on to x, y & z was more toxic to my relationship with God and to my character than I even realized. I wanted the courage to not only *survive*; I wanted the courage to *thrive*.

I admit I didn't really feel any big burst of love or repentance when Vaughan chose to forgive me. It was not until I was ready to take ownership for where I went wrong and stop blaming others and God for my pain that I was ready to be obedient and take that first step forward. Accepting forgiveness. There's that flashing yellow warning sign again! Faith really is scary. Trusting in something you can't see feels much like walking in the dark.

But how could I leave that life of bondage and sinful attraction behind? When I attempted to, all I heard in my mind was: "You'll never amount to anything. Who do you think you are? You'll never be able to change. You're not worthy of God's love and forgiveness. Vaughan deserves better than you." These thoughts plagued my mind and threatened to hold me back. Actually, in all human thinking, I *didn't* deserve forgiveness. None of us do.

How many times did I long to just place my fingers on the CTRL-Z keys and make everything *better*. Simply not possible! Rather, I was slowly learning to trust in the Lord with all my heart and lean not on my own understanding; I was acknowledging Him, and He was directing my paths. Proverbs 3:5-6 (NIV)

When I read these words from Romans 5:20: *"But where sin increased, grace increased all the more" (NIV)*, I think about all the grace that Vaughan has shown me. I'm in full agreement that the bigger our mess, the more God's love and grace is evident! Walking by faith gets easier when you trust the One leading you. If I was still hanging on to the pain I felt when I lost my health, or when Vaughan left for the business trip just hours after we lost our babies, I would have blocked us both from more healing and freedom.

Some people ask me if Vaughan and I really and truly have forgiven each other? Without hesitation, I can tell you that Vaughan and I say that our love today is stronger than the day we said "I do." We actually consider each other best friends. And in case there is any doubt, you're about to get a glimpse into the window of his heart as I share the *Foreword* he wrote for my first book. You'll see that we are living far past just the act of forgiveness and are living in the "more" that God had intended for us.

> *My life was changed when I met Vahen. I knew we were a perfect match and it wasn't only because our names were so similar! We both shared many common interests and beliefs—one of which was in the deep friendship and fellowship of a personal God.*
>
> *I don't think my life is all that extra-ordinary. Bad things happen to everyone—everyone has a story. Before I was married to Vahen, a co-worker took me aside and told me there is no shame in backing out of my wedding plans—my situation had changed and I should re-evaluate my commitment to this girl. Although their concern was with good intentions, I couldn't accept their perspective that my life would be over if I married this girl in a wheelchair. People say that I have such a great testimony because I was willing to make a difficult decision and stick by a person who just had her world pulled out from under her. Even though I didn't know why something like this would happen to Vahen or me, I believe God is in control of everything and Vahen was still the same person I fell in love with.*
>
> *When Vahen first came to me and told me she was writing her story, I asked her why. What do we have to share? We're not*

perfect or have everything figured out. We've struggled financially, spiritually and emotionally. Do we really need to tell the world about our life, our mistakes, and our challenges? Personally, I'm not interested in being the centre of attention, but I accept that God gave her a desire to write her story, and over the years I've never seen someone more dedicated or determined to complete this enormous task. When I finally read her first draft earlier this year, it dug up a lot of forgotten emotions and memories. With tears in my eyes, I had to thank Vahen for staying with me as well through these rough times. We both had to take responsibility for actions and opportunities missed. I guess this is what makes relationships so real!

Life is defined by our experiences and, while no one enjoys a bad experience, they happen to all of us. In this book Vahen shares how she was able to overcome these struggles and change her life story into one of joy and encouragement. I'm proud of Vahen's determination and accomplishments and she is an inspiration even to me. I endorse this book![2]

As everyone does, Vaughan and I have a story. Ours isn't finished yet. It is still ongoing, and we are still growing. But the journey from where we started to where we are now can definitely be summed up in one word: GRACE!

This reminder of the grace I've received from Vaughan never loses its emotional affect on my heart. It gets me every time. Even as I've added his words to this chapter and re-read it, I had to stop and wipe the tears from my eyes. Those were tears not from still carrying shame or guilt, but because I am simply overwhelmed by his unconditional love. But also, I realize that there are many out there just like me. Did I deserve such love and forgiveness after the pain I caused him? No! None of us do. That is exactly my point.

What is different now? The answer is directly related to what I have chosen to do about forgiveness. If I had chosen to disobey and let unforgiveness sit in my heart or if I had refused to accept Vaughan's

---

2 Vaughan King, *Going Farther, Experience the Power and Love of God That Turns Tragedy into Triumph*, (VKM Publishing 2016), Foreword, xiii-xiv.

forgiveness, I could not move forward. But I did make that choice and I am living a transformed life of freedom with the mindset that it doesn't matter what your circumstances are or how hard things get, you can always be free. I am free to have joy in the midst of my pain. I am free to love when the world tells me its okay to hate. I am free to have peace when my world gets turned upside down and everything points to chaos.

The story of my newfound confidence and freedom was not an easy road. It was not void of pain or suffering, but rather it was a path of self-sacrifice, tough choices, and perseverance. Freedom and contagious courage are possible, and you can do it; but you can't do it in your own strength. That understanding is foundational to moving forward. "Withholding or refusing forgiveness results in pain—the kind that can become a toxin in our soul that will stunt our health & vitality."[3]

Unforgiveness, I understand, might be another trigger for many and might be unbearable. Trust me; Vaughan and I both understand. A real-life "CTRL-Z" takes time.

When Vaughan and I started over, even with God's help and Vaughan's support, I battled my demons for a long time before I could say I was free. Please also understand that forgiveness doesn't always mean a return to the same type of relationship. "Forgiveness is giving up the hope of a better past."[4] That was something *else* that held me back for a long time and made it difficult to let go of unforgiveness. However, for Vaughan and me, it wasn't just returning to the same relationship; it was entering something even better. Better past? No. Better future! Yes!

In each step I have learned that no matter where I am in my journey, it all comes down to those same three things which have been emphasized before: unreserved obedience, walking when you can't see, and discipline! Ouch the "D" word. But if you are ready, sit here in this atmosphere and allow yourself some time to feel God's love meeting you where you are. Imagine God sitting next to you and being with you in your pain. Let His love displace

---

3 Shirley Thiessen, *The Little Black Funeral Dress - Five Things I Wish I Had Known About Grief*, page 18 (Tellwell Talent 2018)

4 Lily Tomlin, https://www.goodreads.com/quotes/87427-forgiveness-means-giving-up-all-hope-for-a-better-past (Online 2021, January)

the pain of the circumstances and inaccurate conclusions that are taking up space in your heart. You can answer this question now or come back later. But ask yourself: Is there an area in your life where you need a "CTRL-Z?" On a scale of 1 – 10, how free is your heart?

0 --------------------------- **5** --------------------------------- **10**

10 means *I'm totally free* and 0 means: there ain't no way in _____ I'm forgiving _____.

1 - could mean: I don't even want to entertain the idea of forgiving. However, I am willing to consider that *one* day, if there's a mountain-moving miracle, I might consider the idea.

I might be an ordained minister, but I promise you I will not judge you if your notes get a little colourful with the expression of your hurt and frustration regarding some very painful life struggles. Trust me, God is not offended with our very real emotion to our very real life problems.

As you take this journey with me, I pray that you will ask God to help you face your fears and find the courage to forgive. If you are not ready to go there yet, that's okay. Just please book-mark this section and come back when you are ready.

And if there are any areas for which you need a "do over," remember that "CTRL-Z" takes time! The investment of faith, obedience, and discipline may seem challenging, but you'll also discover the beauty of the CTRL-Z in *your* life.

Chapter 3

Recycled Pain

Breaking past denial and rebuilding our marriage led us to the startling acknowledgment of other losses that had always remained under the surface.

It doesn't matter who you are, what position you hold, what race or religion you are, or what physical abilities you have, you are not exempt from the tragedies of loss. Neither are you exempt from the awful side effects such as fear, feelings of unworthiness, and self-doubt.

Unfortunately, they are no respecter of persons. These are things that affect us all at some point. If we don't acknowledge and accept the *process* that is a necessary part of healing, we can never be free of the things that hold us back. However, my question is: "If it's true that all these things are unavoidable, what do we do with all this pain and suffering?" I believe the bigger question is, "What can God do with all this pain and suffering?"

I would like to speak from my life experience and say that He *recycles* it. For Vaughan and me, it was only after our marriage was restored to a measure of satisfaction for both of us that we realized we had missed the whole process of grieving our losses from the disease. On one occasion when Vaughan and I were in a marriage counseling session the counselor said, "So you've lost a baby and you have now acknowledged that grief. That's great, but have you ever really *mourned the loss of your health?* I was speechless and didn't even know how to respond. I thought we were there to talk about rebuilding our marriage; I never would have linked the marriage breakdown to the *loss of my health.*

Yet, that one question clearly indicated that the loss of my physical mobility was another thing I needed to address before I could heal and love again. Yes, after the virus hit, we had moved forward with the necessary choices and the required physical therapy. However, the necessity of *grieving our losses* was overshadowed by this intense activity. I believe we were stuck somewhere between the stage of shock and denial. We were so focused on the immediate threat and the medical prognosis. Every effort was being poured into beating the odds of this diagnosis and being the "exception" to the bleak future that was predicted. But what about those real *losses* for both of us? We continued with our lives the best we knew how. We got married as we had planned and stumbled on through different phases of adjustment.

People always say: "Never make a major decision after a death." And while you might be thinking, "Vahen, no one died," I was absorbing the loss of my health and my independence without even being aware of the deep unspoken mourning. And I was in complete denial. I was living like this big iceberg—if people could only see all the mess that was underneath! "There are no shortcuts to healing, no magic solution, I have found something— Someone—far better. God himself. When God gets in the middle of life's mess, bad becomes good."[1] Genesis 50:20 tells us that what was meant for "bad" God will use for "good." My creative summary of that would be that God was saying, "Let me recycle that pain. Let me create something beautiful." I had no idea that I was on the track of recycling my pain.

When you first hear my story from beginning to end you get to see the "happy ending." You can get caught up in the romance of "he stayed" but miss the depth of the recycling *process*. This is why I have chosen to go back there with you and take you through it. For true change and healing to occur, we had to acknowledge our losses and understand the process needed to go *through them*. This is commonly understood as "the grieving process" but doesn't always involve a funeral and a casket. Losses such as we *both* experienced required a process in order for transformation to be possible. Yes, I was mourning the loss of my physical independence and having to now cope with all the limitations that came with that. My pattern of denial was continuing to shape my life. Yes, I was in a wheelchair with vastly reduced mobility, but that was just the tip of the iceberg. Even more

---

1 Max Lucado, *God Will Carry You Through, Ultimate Victory,* YouVersion devotional, Day 8

so, I was mourning the loss of "me." All that I had envisioned my life to be was slipping away. In order for God to recycle my pain, I had to let it go. It's hard to believe that what I thought had destroyed me would ultimately lead me to more courage and freedom than I ever knew existed. It's because of that discovery that I am committed to the reality that hope can be ignited in the darkest places.

Vaughan and I have both suffered tremendous loss; but he wouldn't really tell you he's "missing out." That's just another part of the amazing man that he is. There are times even today when Vaughan looks at me and says, "Sweetie, we are better because of you." However, the fact still remains that we both suffered tremendous loss. Plus, we both healed in our own way. By now I'm sure you'll all agree: When God recycles pain, He does it with amazing detail and truly personalizes the process.

Allow me to introduce you to a dear friend, Shirley Thiessen. She is another incredible person with an amazing story of courage. She also allowed God to come in and recycle her unbearable pain. Shirley vulnerably wrote about her life-altering loss in her book, *The Little Black Funeral Dress—Five Things I Wish I Had Known About Grief.* Here's a window into Shirley's story as she tells it. Her insights are also valuable as we consider recycling our pain and growing through the process.

"In 2012 my husband Carey and I experienced what we considered a parent's worst nightmare: the death of a child. Only 12 days after celebrating our son's wedding, we had the devastating task of planning his funeral. Our son, Jordan, died tragically in a workplace accident.

While my grief changes from year to year, I will never be over it. Not until I reach Heaven. But in the meantime, I have been experiencing firsthand how God is able to recycle my pain for His good purpose. And I know He wants to do that for you, too. With our participation, God will re-purpose our pain. The question is, will we let Him?

No matter what world-view you hold, I would hazard to guess that you may be grieving a painful loss right now. It's the reality of being part of the human race. Like me, some of you are grieving the death of a loved one. For some, it's the loss of your marriage or the loss of a friendship. For others, it's the loss of your health, or the loss of a job, or even the loss of a dream.[2]

While absorbing the horrendous nightmare of my son's death, there is one truth which has been imprinted on my heart as a result of my history with God. It is this: Jesus is my foundation, my purpose and my living hope. While my husband and my kids are at the epicenter of the people I love most dearly, they are not my only reason for living. They are not the ultimate source of my joy. Only God can satisfy that role.[3]

CS Lewis wisely puts it this way, "Don't let your happiness depend on something you may lose." You may lose a child, a spouse, your health, your job, your reputation, your dearest friend, or you can even lose your mind, but God promises that HE will never leave you or forsake you. He is our reason for living."

Personally, I have found that God promises to recycle our pain for His good purpose, as we participate.

You may be wondering, "So, why should I care about recycling pain? Consider this: Our pain can become a toxin in our soul that will stunt our health & vitality. We all know people who could be described as "stuck" in their grief. They're not easy to be around. They carry an air of cynicism and hopelessness. They might still be functioning in society, but they aren't really living with any sense of joy or purpose. The pain and suffering they have experienced has crushed their spirit. For a time, this was a description of me. But gradually with God's grace and compassionate friends, I have experienced a hope-filled story that is giving others courage to trust God with their painful loss.

Because our grief-avoidant society rarely talks about death and grief, I've chosen to leverage what God has taught me through my painful grief journey and use it to help others navigate their loss in healthy ways."[4]

When our world gets turned upside-down or we get hurt by others, it is predictable that depression and mistrust can become the "new normal." When we face prolonged challenges or impossible situations, the trauma

---

2 Shirley Thiessen, *The Little Black Funeral Dress - Five Things I Wish I Had Known About Grief*, (Tellwell Talent 2018), 17-18.

3 Ibid., 38.

4 Ibid., 30-31.

and fear result in emotional paralysis. Not knowing where to turn for help, we often remain stuck. How is it even possible to move forward and be free? How you choose to respond will determine if you move forward in freedom or remain paralyzed by fear.

I shared all that to allow you to really see the *process* of healing and moving forward. Healing comes in different timings and in different ways. And often healing comes in ways we don't even realize or think we need. There are 7 stages of loss and grief that we travel through. The stages of the process need to be acknowledged in order for us to keep moving forward. You never want to rush this process, nor do you want to stay too long in one stage. Your journal notes and record of your feelings attached to events will serve as a road map. This is why I've encouraged you to journal as you are reading this book so we can share our discoveries and transformations.

Your journal can be of great benefit to you. If you become "lost" or sidetracked on the journey, the words you either write or quote from someone else can provide hope that the destination is possible. Without hope we know it is nearly impossible to survive. This is why I'm believing that something learned here will act as a tool in *your* survival guide. It may take each of us a different length of time to reach healing, but if we keep finding the strength and courage to push forward, we will get through it.

In the following graph it becomes very clear that in each of the stages of the grief process there will be what seem to be escape options one might choose instead of moving forward. Like me when I was more comfortable in my pain than the discomfort of working through infidelity. There are emotions that we experience at each stage. And, of course, these stages do not happen in a straight line. Do you have pain that needs to be recycled? Allow yourself to sit undistracted. May I suggest spending time looking at the 7 stages and making notes in your journal on the things to consider from Shirley's journey. This is a safe space for your reflections.

This second model, *How People Feel Through the Stages of Change*, presents another helpful guide, because it shows how change does not always move in a straight line. Many times, even though we are actually making progress, we may find ourselves circling back to the intensity of our experience. However, as indicated here, change *is possible,* and change is *happening.*

> Dr. Kübler-Ross refined her model to include seven stages of loss. The seven stages of loss model is a more in-depth analysis of the components of the grief process. These seven stages include shock, denial, anger, bargaining, depression, testing, and acceptance. Kübler-Ross added the two steps as an extension of the grief cycle. In the shock phase, you feel paralyzed and emotionless. In the testing stage, you try to find realistic solutions for coping with the loss and rebuilding your life.[5]

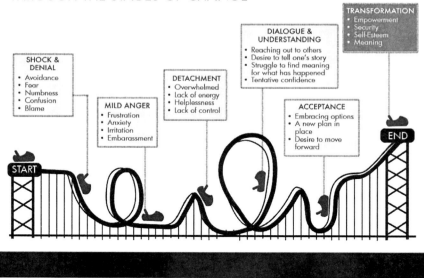

HOW PEOPLE FEEL THROUGH THE STAGES OF CHANGE

● **The Burnie Group**

SHOCK & DENIAL
- Avoidance
- Fear
- Numbness
- Confusion
- Blame

MILD ANGER
- Frustration
- Anxiety
- Irritation
- Embarassment

DETACHMENT
- Overwhelmed
- Lack of energy
- Helplessness
- Lack of control

DIALOGUE & UNDERSTANDING
- Reaching out to others
- Desire to tell one's story
- Struggle to find meaning for what has happened
- Tentative confidence

ACCEPTANCE
- Embracing options
- A new plan in place
- Desire to move forward

TRANSFORMATION
- Empowerment
- Security
- Self-Esteem
- Meaning

START   END

6

Before we move on, I want to acknowledge that while forgiveness isn't listed in either *The Seven Stages of Grief model*, or *How People Feel Through*

---

5 The modified Kübler-Ross model, *The Seven Stages of Grief*, https://www.betterhelp.com/advice/grief/understanding-the-stages-of-grief/ (Online 2021, January)

6 The Burnie Group, *The Five Stages of Change*, https://burniegroup.com/5-stages-of-change/ (Online 2021, January)

the Stages of Change graph, my personal, though unprofessional opinion, is that forgiveness is most definitely an underlying factor through each and every stage of this process. Only then can we allow God to recycle our pain.

Chapter 4

Where Does This Fit?

Sometimes I think of my life like a giant puzzle. Over time God gives me glimpses of the bigger picture of my life's purpose. And, with each piece of the puzzle I receive, I gain more insight that builds this unexplainable excitement inside me. It's an excitement for what He's doing *and* what He's going to do.

In contrast, there have been many times when I couldn't see where the pieces I have been given are supposed to fit. I think about the events in my life since transverse myelitis took my independence and nearly destroyed me, my marriage, and everything I valued. There were many pieces that didn't seem to fit. I had made such a total mess of what I was given and then wondered how God could possibly use this. As I started piecing my life together it looked nothing like the image I had envisioned for my life. It didn't make sense, and at times just looked like a scattered mess. That's when it gets really hard. But that's when God would challenge me to really trust Him with *my "mad"* and *my frustration* as He moves the pieces of my life around to make them fit.

Another example of a "piece" I couldn't understand, and most definitely *never* would have chosen, was when we lost my father-in-law to cancer in March of 2017. My father-in-law was a close mentor and strong believer in who I was meant to be, even when I didn't see it in myself. I always enjoyed listening to what Father John had to say. Whether it was his "off the wall" sense of humor or his conversations that made me dream bigger, even when we didn't agree, he always had my full attention. Listening to him tell about his *many* amazing missionary adventures was a delight. (He even wrote a book filled with these short stories if you are intested in reading it yourself)[1]. But truthfully, some of my favorite times with Father John were when we'd be sitting in the same room trying to work, but I'd be talking his ear off while he would *always* graciously appear interested.

I saw Father John as a big piece of my life's puzzle and such an example of how the Lord works through our relationships to complete who we are to be. After he was gone, I was left thinking, "How can my puzzle ever be complete if such a big piece is missing?"

Around the time when we all went to Africa together on a speaking trip, I felt God also planted in my heart that I would be on a world stage to share my story. At first, I thought it was impossible. How am I going to be on a world stage? The only way that made sense to me was with my father-in-law of course. He's a missionary and has been to over 75 countries. There's the world stage. So, after the first year of speaking and launching the initial season of ministry, Vaughan and I were beginning to consider joining him on some of his adventures. We could envision that we'd start traveling with him to fulfill the dream and vision I felt God gave me.

So, when he passed, I was devastated for the obvious reasons but also was left with the question, "What now?" And you can be sure that I was being fed lying thoughts such as, " If you were wrong about your world stage, what else are you wrong about? Maybe God doesn't really have this plan for you to impact the world as you think."

Allow me to share something with you that I found in the midst of planning my father-in-law's memorial. In those hours of dealing with this loss and trying to make sense of it all, I came across something he wrote in his journal...

"Don't Waste Your Suffering"

Life won't get easier.
Learn to accept disappointments, suffering, and incalculable loss.
On some levels, life may become easier, but the fact is, you'll

---

1 John & Laura King, *Off the Wall & On His Pedestal: Escapades of a Maverick Missionary* (VKM Publishing 2018)

weather one crisis only to face another.
Life will never become void of pain, discouragement, or periods of suffering.
But remember, these are the tools of your Lord to transform you.
So lean into them to discover a new aspect of Jesus.
*A crisis is an **unwelcomed** opportunity for growth.*
So, don't waste your suffering."

The moment I read his words "Don't waste your suffering," I knew that statement would be part of his legacy that will live on through my husband and I. And while I didn't have all the answers, I knew that God was providing the strength I needed in that moment to keep going in faith. I knew I could trust Him. Continuing on was really hard, but continue on I did.

I'll let you in on a little secret about God. More often than not, He will make amazing things happen through our little decisions. He'll provide an *opportunity* and it might seem good or bad to us at the time, but how we embrace that choice makes all the difference into a powerful outcome.

Four months after Father John passed, a friend of mine suggested I should apply to join the Miss Wheelchair Canada pagent with her that fall in Vancouver, British Columbia. At first I balked at the idea, with excuses like: "Isn't that pretty vain?" or "I'm about to become an ordained minister, how does this ever benefit my ministry?", but my parents and husband supported the idea. I jumped in with a thrill in my heart and the next thing I knew, I was winning Miss Wheelchair Canada and heading to Poland for the Miss Wheelchair World pageant. Who would have ever believed that I would win a beauty pageant and be crowned Miss Kindness on a world stage in Poland? Then I was invited to do T.V. interviews and speak at school and community events across Canada to share my story. I don't know about you, but this blew my mind. (And, definitely muted the taunting arguments from the enemy!) I am sure you can see how we have to trust God with all the pieces we can't understand.

Father John's absence no longer felt like the gaping hole leaving us incomplete. Rather, I realized how enriched my life had been through him. And, that didn't end with his home-going. As I am in the middle of writing this book, I experienced someone praying the most beautiful prayer over my life. The individual prayed many great words of life and encouragement, but one thing that really struck my heart as he prayed was that I totally felt he was describing Father John. I was so blessed I had to tell him that the way he acknowledges my life and how I live was exactly how I have heard people describe "Paw." The tears just started falling as I had just this beautiful moment of feeling that I am carrying John's legacy and I know he would be so proud.

Yes, of course, I still miss him. And, at times I wish he could see me *dreaming bigger and pushing others to do the same!* But, like those moments when I discovered the treasure that he had written and the prayer of a dear friend, I have seen my faith and courage grow stronger as I have learned to trust when I don't understand.

Navigating the incalculable losses or unwelcome circumstances is never an easy process. But for me, I have found that all the events in my life—both good and bad—formed the big picture of my life.

As I reflect back to May 30, 1999, when transverse myelitis came onto the landscape of my life, I thought my dreams of making a positive impact on the world had ended. That image of how I saw my life was no longer clear. However, what I thought was the end of my dreams actually set me on a path to receiving more than I ever dreamed possible. These are puzzle pieces I would *never* have selected as part of my life, but I choose to let God use them for His glory. I know now that if I am never tested, I will never know what I am capable of. And if I don't learn to trust God, I'll never know what *He's* capable of.

Trying to understand where all my "pieces" fit in the *process* is indeed a steep learning curve for me. I have experienced many lessons about surrender and self sacrifice. When they are mixed with *lots* of love, patience, faith, and obedience, you get the most amazing finished product. And the result: you gain unexplainable peace, defiant joy, and a courage that is contagious.

God's perspective on my puzzle pieces has given me the courage to lean on His strength and power—not my own. And, as a result, I'm looking forward with *great expectation* to what *else* God has for me. I am going to fight like a warrior with the strength of my Heavenly Father. Yes, a giant slayer in training. And, in the face of fear, insecurities, and self doubt, I will choose courage and trust Him. Let me share a poem here of how the "unlikely pieces" fit into the fabric of our lives.

"The Father and The Child"

The Father spoke:
Come, child, let us journey together.
Where shall we go, Father?
To a distant land, another kingdom.
So the journey will be long?
Yes, we must travel every day.
When will we reach our destination?
At the end of your days.
And who will accompany us?
Joy and sorrow.
Must Sorrow travel with us?
Yes, she is necessary to keep you close to Me.
But I want only Joy.
It is only with Sorrow that you will know true Joy.
What must I bring?
A willing heart to follow me.
What shall I do on the journey?
There is only one thing that you must do----Stay close to Me.
Let nothing distract you. Always keep your eyes on Me.
And what will I see?
You will see My glory.
And what will I know?
You will know my heart.
The Father stretched out His hand.
The child, knowing the great love her Father had for her,
Placed her hand in His and began her journey.[2]

---

2 Cynthia Heald, The Father and the Child, *Becoming a Woman of Excellence*, 30th Anniversary Edition, (NavPress in alliance with Tyndale House, Colorado Springs, Co, 2016), Introduction

Do you have some mismatched or disfigured puzzle pieces in front of *you*? Are you struggling to know where they fit? Maybe you are mad at God? Or perhaps you are frustrated and are at a place where you have concluded that God has forgotten you or that He just doesn't care. Pause and take time to write out your thoughts about the pieces of your life that don't make sense. I don't know what the future will bring for you, but I pray that you will trust God completely to make *all* your pieces *fit*.

_____

_____

_____

_____

_____

_____

_____

_____

_____

_____

_____

_____

Section 2

Preparing for a Life of Courage

You Say

*I keep fighting voices in my mind that say I'm not enough
Every single lie that tells me I will never measure up
Am I more than just the sum of every high and every low
Remind me once again just who I am because I need to know*

*You say I am loved when I can't feel a thing
You say I am strong when I think I am weak
And you say I am held when I am falling short
And when I don't belong, oh You say I am Yours
And I believe, Oh, I believe
What You say of me, I believe*

*The only thing that matters now is everything You think of me
In You I find my worth, in You I find my identity*

*Taking all I have, and now I'm laying it at Your feet
You have every failure, God, You have every victory*

*You say I am loved when I can't feel a thing
You say I am strong when I think I am weak
You say I am held when I am falling short
When I don't belong, oh You say I am Yours
And I believe[1]*

---

1 You Say, Album: Look Up Child, Writer(s): Paul Mabury, Lauren Daigle & Jason Ingram. WMG (on behalf of Centricity Music/12Tone); LatinAutor - UMPG, , (C) 2018

I Am Courageous!

If you were asked, "Are *you* courageous?" On a scale of 1-10, where would you land?

0 --------------------------- 5 --------------------------------- 10

Did you know that even if you scored a 1, you can still claim the statement, "I am courageous."

Before you doubt my reasoning for making such a statement, let's have a visit together.

In the introduction I invited you to journey with me through this book with journal and pen in hand. Have you done that? If not, it's certainly not too late to begin. If so, then I am sure you've had some very interesting (and helpful) entries through these chapters. I'm also guessing there have been some pretty brave discoveries in your self-reflections. Either way, I would like for us to stop again and reflect on Section One. If there were things you want to go back and revisit, please allow time here to do so. I've brought a few key statements forward and I want you to write down some of the thoughts that come to mind now as we have come this far.

What responses did you have to the statements in Section 1 about "looking deeper than the tip of the iceberg?" Is there more pain under your surface than you are willing to let people see? Or are you wishing you had the courage to allow someone to see your pain, or to love you where you are? "What's underneath" was devastating when I was trapped in my pain. In my growth with God "what's underneath" takes on a whole new meaning. Watch for that as we continue into the following chapters.

When we began our journey, I also asked you what giants you wanted to see fall in your life. Did you write them down? Well now I want to invite you to write down the name of one person you would be open to sharing with.

_____

And when you have time, I would even suggest writing out your thoughts in a letter. You will not believe the healing that will come just by writing out something that you've kept buried or have tried to hide. Vaughan and I received even more healing just by writing my first book. Maybe you have some news for your spouse or someone close that could do some serious damage to a lot of people or just yourself. While I'm not really advocating that you "go public," it's likely time to share it in a safe place that's confidential. That step of reaching out is indeed a courageous one. However, without this step, your healing and freedom could be severely delayed. I pray that even today you will see a glimpse of that hope, freedom, or courage you have been so desperately looking for.

There were other statements I'm sure that you might want to revisit. (You can find statements like these and more in the "Reflect & Review" section at the back of the book.) I just chose a few.

Faulty Thinking Blocks Courage

Faulty thinking held me back for a long time from the courage and freedom I am now experiencing. What really is courage? Courage is having the mental or moral strength to venture, persevere, and withstand danger, fear, or difficulty[1]. I can definitely relate to that. Maybe you think courage and freedom are just abstracts that seem far-fetched and only attained by the very elite. Or just a pipe dream that one can only hope to attain. I get it, because that was totally me.

While there are many sources for "faulty thinking" that can creep

---

1 Merriam – Webster Incorporated, merriam-webster.com/dictionary (Online 2021, January)

into our life's narrative, they all share the common goal to draw inaccurate conclusions about ourselves. Self-perspective matters. When we give into negative self-talk we are prone to accumulate faulty thinking as our take-away from all the challenges in our lives. And, while I don't have this all figured out yet, I have come to believe: "You can't always control what happens to you, but you *can* control how you respond!"

The fears and insecurities of my faulty thinking that I had to push through even in 2019 and into 2020 were, at times, unbearable. And while you might be thinking of the fear regarding COVID-19 in 2020, for me it was actually about so much more. As November 2019 began, I had just returned from a month-long speaking tour in Newfoundland Labrador. As you can well imagine I was emotionally and physically exhausted. However, as I saw what was ahead for 2020, I was also excited to be involved with the second "Hope Talks" conference that was created by my amazing friend Connie Jakab. I celebrated with her that it had grown from the "first ever" event, to now 3 locations in just one year. While Connie was hoping to be in all 3 locations, she *was* only one person and it was just not possible. What a surprise when she asked me to lead the conference in the Edmonton location. It was a true honour! I was like, "*Totally!* I'm in!" However, it wasn't long before I was overwhelmed by the task I had just agreed to. Add to the fact that I was still recovering from exhaustion didn't help. I felt that I was in way over my head.

I began to experience all of the old patterns of self-doubt and insecurity. I feared I would fail and the conference would be a total flop. Not only would I be letting Connie down, but I would look like a complete idiot in my hometown. Feeling the pressure, I was at times bawling my eyes out and even hoping that we could cancel the event. And, I am embarrassed to say, I even suggested it might need to be cancelled. My hesitation in this had nothing to do with not wanting to be a part of this incredible Hope Movement. It was simply my insecurity regarding my ability to execute it.

As we talked it out Connie said, "Vahen, you were made for this. I don't know what's happening, but I believe that this is an attack on your courage. You need to be confident in who you are." There were many other "pep talks" along the way. I finally faced my fear and just committed wholeheartedly to the fact that it was happening and I was leading. I pulled myself together and pushed through. So, trust me when I tell you that the excitement of being a part of something that was so much bigger than me returned once I was no longer paralyzed by fear.

So, there we were, only two days away from the conference. I had a meet and greet at my house with all the speakers and workshop leaders, etc. to go over the order of the day. I remember sitting in the room with the leaders thinking, "Wow, I'm actually leading this group of high-quality leaders and I'm not afraid." And, those thoughts were not once countered by other the voices in my head saying, "You don't belong here." I was actually seeing myself as able to take this role. People may see me as a confident leader, but this challenge was definitely "next level" since I was leading those who were way more qualified and experienced in the field of mental health than me.

January 29, 2020, arrived and the conference happened. I had never emceed before, but I had the time of my life. Jesse Lipscombe, who co-emceed with me, was an amazing partner who really helped validate me and boost my confidence that day. The feedback from the conference was just way more than we ever expected. Many thanks go to the amazing team who helped pull it all off. Of special note was Bob Jones, who received my many "mayday" calls. He was also a great support in helping me see that I *could* do this. My amazing friend Adrienne Fudge, with "Help The Help Inc," was also key in making sure this event was a success. Honestly, without her, this event actually wouldn't have happened.

There is so much more I could say about that event and the many people who helped make it possible, but what I'll say is that I am so thrilled that I pushed past my fear and chose courage. When I saw how God gave me the courage to do that, I was challenged and changed." Wow, God, if you helped me do that, what *else* can I do." Facing your fears and conquering them really does change your self-perception.

About a month after the conference on February 23, 2020, God showed me a picture of a dam about to burst. As the water was gushing through the dam, it was breaking apart even more. I sensed Him saying, "You are bursting into a new season. And in this next season there will be mindsets and other things break off of you that will catapult you forward." He continued, "I want to give you new courage in this next season. You can't carry the insecurities you had in the past with you where you are going." Then He showed me that when that dam is fully broken, the water will rush right through and will not stop flowing. He showed me that I represented that dam. The water flowing through me is His strength. I continued to hear Him speak to me: "When My strength is running through you, there will be no limitations for you in the Spirit. When you are walking in My strength, you have nothing to fear and you will be unstoppable."

When I started writing *Contagious Courage*, I will tell you that my courage was tested in unimaginable ways. So, it was no surprise that I felt that this book would be written from my prayer time. I knew that God wanted to give me the courage to share what's in my heart, but I needed to spend time with Him to receive that strength. I told my husband I felt this book would be birthed on my knees. Looking back and seeing what I went though with the Hope conference and many other things that threatened to destroy my confidence since that time, I realized just how many times I would come back to Him for guidance and strength. I knew I *needed* the courage that He desired to give me, to truly express what's in my heart and not hold back out of fear or insecurities. I wanted people to truly see me. I believe that when you truly see me, you will truly see Him. If I wrote *Contagious Courage* and left out how God was the source of my courage, I wouldn't be true to myself.

Why would this even be an issue? You see, since the release of my first book and winning the Miss Wheelchair Canada title, doors were really opening up. I was speaking in schools and other community events where you can't really talk about Jesus. In those settings I knew that *was* appropriate. I actually believe people see Him much more through how I live my life than by what I say. But when writing this book, I was torn. Actually, I was terrified. Again! This indecision was a roadblock for about a month, maybe longer.

Finally, one morning I went to God and said something like this to Him: "Okay, you need to help me here, God. What if schools close and I don't get invited in? What if churches close because they don't accept that we need more love and relationship and less religion? How do I move past this?" This was what He spoke into my heart that day: "If schools close to you, it will be okay. If churches close on you, it will also be okay. Even if Canada closes its doors to you, the world will receive the message you have to share." I will tell you I was still terrified, but a weight lifted off of me. Even if I was rejected, I was okay with that because I was confident that by faith, I was being obedient to do what God was asking of me.

About 3 months into the COVID-19 pandemic I was sharing this with a friend. Her response was, "Vahen, schools *did* close to you! Churches *did* close to you. And literally everything got shut down in Canada and across the globe; but you have access to the world like never before." As soon as she said that my tears began to fall. Now I understood what God meant. He hadn't been telling me I would be an outcast no one wanted to hear. Rather, He was giving me a word to let me know that He was still in control and that I could share my heart without fear or intimidation.

You see, when we limit ourselves or our capacity to what *we* think *we* can accomplish, we will likely be paralyzed with fear when we are faced with circumstances outside of our control.

"Courage is not the absence of fear but choosing to act in spite of fear."[2]

Building Blocks to Courage

Allow me to illustrate this from some more of my (risk-taking!) experiences. When I tell people that I've jumped out of an airplane, they say, "Wow, you're so courageous." And, rightly so. That's pretty brave. But the truth is that I get the same reaction when I tell people I drive myself around or do my own groceries. Some may consider it more courageous to be able to drive a vehicle although I am still in my wheelchair than to jump out of an airplane. One day I actually had a lady follow me from the parking lot into a store and say, "I just saw you get out of that car. Did you drive yourself?" When I said with a chuckle, "Yes, that was me," you should have seen her

---

2 Bruce Wilkinson, *The Dream Giver: Following Your God Given Destiny,* (Multnomah Publishers Sisters, Oregon 2003), 93.

reaction. With her eyes wide open and with tears, she said, "Wow, you are one brave lady." She then continued to tell me reasons why she didn't feel so brave and how seeing me that day had really encouraged her. We chatted a little, we hugged, and went about our day.

So, don't automatically eliminate yourself from the category of "courageous." Yes, courage can describe those who face extreme danger or difficulties without fear. However, what you may have to do every day in the face of your fears, or even something you do that just seems to come naturally to you, can be equally, if not more, courageous!

I wonder why we find it so hard to tell ourselves that we are courageous? I think about all the things I have shared with you, and yet, I struggle with it. So trust me, I understand. But the difference now is that I shut fear down quicker. I needed to change that mindset, and so do you. I think about what Lisa Bevere said in her book *Strong*: "Strong is not wrong." She said, *"Too often Christian woman are associated with weakness rather than strength. Sometimes religion has taught us to hide rather than to rise. It's true that we are called to be meek, but not weak. Meek is best defined as strength under control"*[3] I could keep quoting from that book, but you'll have to get the book and read it for yourself.

What have you done that you don't think is courageous, but others might? Maybe you think it's a silly question. Yes, it may seem silly, but write it down. Your comments will definitely appear in the map of your life as you navigate your way forward. Like that lady who told me I was courageous simply because she saw me being independent in this wheelchair. I have not always been confident in this chair; but now that I have come to embrace where I am, I can sometimes forget how courageous it can appear to others. And, as I've mentioned before, your words or stories about your courage could be in someone else's survival guide. I say that because most of what was written in my first book and even in this book, would not have been remembered, or even believed, if I didn't have my journal notes to reflect on.

---

3 Lisa Bevere, *Strong: Devotions – To Live a Powerful & Passionate Life*, (Thomas Nelson 2020), 2.

Ditch Your "I Can't" Mentality

Now let me ask you this, "How many times today have you said, "I can't?" Maybe you've told yourself: "I'm not enough!" Or, "I'm not good enough or smart enough to accomplish my dreams." Okay, perhaps you didn't say it quite like that. But maybe it comes out in your everyday responses such as when you say, "I can't wear that; it makes me look fat." Or like when I said, "I can't lead a mental health conference, I am not a health care professional." Recently I told my physiotherapist that I couldn't do something he was asking me to do. His quick response was, "Don't say I can't! You've got to stop that. Maybe you're not doing it like you want to, but that *I can't* business has got to stop." We laughed as I told him about this chapter. How often do we use this negative self-talk over our lives? I'll quote my therapist again for our mutual benefit: "That *I can't* business has got to stop."

While I don't want you to spend a lot of time focused on all the things you say you *can't* do, I do believe it is important to take a mental picture so you can understand where you are. Bruce Wilkinson's book, *The Dream Giver*[4], has been so resourceful to me in learning how to step out and push through fear. I would like to recommend it to you. Now let me also ask you this, "Have you ever had to make a decision about something or face someone and you were terrified at the thought, but, you did it anyway?" *Now that is the definition of courage!*

Consider the following questions. This will help you discover along your journey just how courageous you are.

Write out a time, or times, when you tried a new food. Was that a good or bad experience?

_____

_____

_____

---

4 Bruce Wilkinson, *The Dream Giver: Following Your God Given Destiny,* (Multnomah Publishers Sisters, Oregon 2003)

_____

_____

_____

People who know me also know I am not the adventurous type when it comes to trying new foods. But every so often I'll take the plunge. And, what better place to do this than at the "Taste of Edmonton." Every type of food you can think of, and most every restaurant from Edmonton is represented. I'm not a green tea drinker myself, but I love ice cream. So, I thought I'd try green tea ice cream. I admit it tasted like dirt, but I tried it! Then came the real adventure! Squid rings? I grew up on the east coast, so this shouldn't be that bad, right? No comment! But again, I tried it!

Write out a time when you tried something new that you never thought you would or could do.

_____

_____

_____

_____

_____

_____

I invited a friend to travel with me to Montreal one year when I was invited to speak there. She thought it would be fun to try something new. That's when she told be about this restaurant called ONoir where you eat in the dark. I can't say I had a panic attack, but I was hoping she would change her mind and decide it was too adventurous even for her.

Eating in the dark? How is that even possible? How do you find your food? There is no way you can have hot tea or soup, is there? Never mind that, I'm a klutz even when I can see my food. I thought, "This will be a nightmare." I could write a full chapter on this experience, but let me just say, "I did it, and it was amazing!" It was *very* messy, but it *was* fun! Yes, I ate with my fingers. How else did you think I was going to find the food on my plate? My friend and I laughed so hard, especially when in the pitch dark we tried to clink our glasses attempting to "do cheers" for our bravery.

But the most surprising thing was that it was the best tasting meal I have ever had. Apparently, when your other senses are taken away, your sense of taste is heightened. That's one of the reasons they decided to do this "eating in the dark" restaurant. Oh, I need to circle back here, because the most surprising thing wasn't that it was the best meal ever; rather it was that all the servers were visually impaired. How remarkable to support employment opportunities for this type of disability. Excellent! Anyway, all that to say, I never thought I could eat in the dark! But I did, and it was amazing. And similarly, I *thought* I could never write a book or start my own non-profit organization. I'm telling you guys, most of our limitations *are* self-imposed.

Have you ever tried an extreme sport or done something daring you thought you would never do?

_____

_____

_____

_____

_____

_____

I thought eating in the dark was brave, but sky diving? This was never on my bucket list and the thought alone was terrifying. But, I did it anyway! The thing that shocked me the most was that once I actually made up my mind to do it, the fear factor was settled. As we were on that plane, climbing up to an altitude of 14,000 ft, I said, "*Oh, my word*, this is mind-blowing to me! How bizarre to realize I wasn't afraid; now that's definitely something to write home about!" There is so much more to that story, but let's just say that I realized just how much freedom was awaiting me on the other side of my fear. Check out my YouTube channel for the video. Search for "Do You See

Fear on This Face?" One confession before I move on. When I was first asked to sky dive, I was thinking about the "bragging rights" I'd have. I wanted this on my courage resume. Now, is that considered courageous or just stupid? Depends on who you ask, I guess.

Here's one last question.

Have you ever found yourself standing up for a person who is being bullied?

_____

_____

_____

_____

_____

_____

I did, and, that someone was *me*. I was in grade 7. After 6 years of being picked on, I finally kicked this guy in the ____. There we were, standing in a crowded hallway and my bully was taunting me. He was daring me to kick him in the *you know what*. With everyone watching in anticipation of what I would do, I did it! Let's just say that he didn't bother me *ever* again. He may not have been the only bully I've ever had to face in my life, but he definitely represents them.

Courage comes in all shapes and sizes. But what you will hopefully discover here is that to be honest, the worst experiences (or most terrifying ones) actually make for the best stories and create the bravest warriors.

You are likely much more courageous than you give yourself credit for. What if you started the day by telling yourself you are courageous? What if you understood that you very likely do courageous things every day? But even more importantly, what if you understood that you actually have additional strength available to you that will help you keep stepping up to push past your fear? How much better would you feel? Or, how does it feel to see all the times that you have been and still are being courageous every day?

We are *so* quick to tell ourselves that "we can't" or that we are not brave; but the reality is we *can* and we *are*! For example, maybe you're a single mom who has to work hard everyday to provide for her children. Maybe you are a cancer survivor who had to endure chemo treatments and battle everyday with the fears of "Will I live or die?" Or maybe you just had a bleak diagnosis and you are looking for the strength you never thought you would need? The fact that you are still here, I would say, means you should consider yourself brave and courageous. And while we don't all have life- threatening situations to face everyday, you need to know that you are strong *despite* what you feel.

Remember: your faith is not determined by what you see or how you feel. When you choose to trust God *in spite* of what you see and feel you have access to much more strength and courage than you ever thought possible. The journey to freedom is not *one big* step, but *many little* ones. The more we understand about the journey ahead, the more prepared and equipped we will be to face it. Many times we don't even realize we're being held back. Fears, insecurities, negative self-talk, and social pressures make it easy to accept these limitations as normal. Before we move on, I trust you have discovered that this journey will require faith, obedience, and discipline to walk out our life of courage and freedom. Please know that you are not alone in your challenges. Don't forget: "Courage isn't about not being afraid; rather it is about not letting fear control you!"[5] Say it with me, "*I am courageous!*"

---

5 Bruce Wilkinson, *The Dream Giver: Following Your God Given Destiny,* (Multnomah Publishers Sisters, Oregon 2003), 93.

Chapter 6

Knowing is Only Half the Battle

Do you like to travel? Just for fun, let me ask you this: "How many of you over-pack?" Are you the type to go over every possible mood or weather change and choose an outfit to accommodate? Or do you pack as little as possible and only the essentials make it into your luggage? Is your philosophy: "If I forget something, I'll buy it there?" I'm sure there are other ways to prepare for a trip, but these are just two extremes that come to mind. What kind of packer are you?

Whether it is for business or pleasure, one thing remains the same no matter what kind of packer you are. *You need to be prepared.* If I'm going to Mexico, I know that I'll be needing sunscreen and light clothing. If I am going on an Antarctic tour, I'll need my parka and warm boots. However, if I am going to Newfoundland Labrador, it's not a stretch to say I could need a parka one day and a spring jacket the next. Whatever the reason or the season for your travel, there would be a certain level of frustration if you don't know how to prepare. Right?

For the record, I am that person who over-packs. Especially when I can't really predict what each day will bring. When I went to Poland for the Miss Wheelchair World beauty pageant in 2017, my sister came with me. I remember admiring her ability to travel with just a carry-on for ten days. Now, I realize that I had gowns and shoes. Oh my—the shoes! How can I possibly choose between my three favorite pairs? And what about my boots! There was no way I could make this trip without the 5 pairs I decided on. My "indecisive self" found this process exciting yet painful. So, I erred on the side of taking almost *everything*! You might be laughing at me and that's okay. But I'm sure you'll agree that packing for something you never had to prepare for before can be unbelievably difficult.

Well, the night of the final gala came. Besides all the obvious excitement of the lights, cameras, and lots of runway action, we were so spoiled. The gifts just kept coming. It was just like Christmas morning. The sad reality was, there was *no way* I was going to get all this loot back to Canada. However, thanks to my sister's *mad-packing* skills, we *were* able to get *almost* everything in my suitcase. Of course, *knowing* that I would have needed the extra space for all these presents would have been most helpful. And I would have avoided leaving behind some things I would rather have kept. Would I have packed less? Or would I have brought the extra luggage bag? Oh, the frustration of not knowing how to prepare properly.

Understanding where you are going and how to prepare for your destination will have a profound impact on your overall well-being and success as you travel. Knowing in advance what you need saves a lot of frustration.

Following Instructions Matters

While being prepared is a major factor in setting yourself up for a successful trip, that still *is* only half the battle. Knowing what to do is still incomplete unless you do it!

How are you with following instructions? With any "guide," whether in written format or if you actually have a tour guide, being obedient to follow instructions is just as important as having the right clothing or accessories for a trip.

One summer after high school I remember planning to go on an all-day trip to the beach with my friends. I wore my cutest two-piece bathing suit and had my sunblock, sunglasses, and food for the day. Yup! I had all the essentials. I usually "lather up" with sunblock before I go out in the sun. After all, I am a redhead, so need I say more? However, I was running late and thought I would do it there. Well, we arrived at the beach, and in the excitement, I forgot to put on my sunblock. Then later, when I *did* remember,

I told myself, "I'm okay, I'll just keep going in the shade when I'm feeling too hot." *WHAT WAS I THINKING?*

Long story short, it was not a pleasant ending to a pleasant day for this girl. By the time I got home I was feeling weak and nearly passing out. I was attempting to get ready to go out with my friends after a day at the beach; but instead, I ended up in an ambulance on route to the hospital. Burnt to a crisp and looking like a lobster, I lay on the hospital bed dehydrated and hooked up to the IV. My only thought was, "Why, didn't I just put on the sunblock like I planned?" And then I was asked how much water I drank throughout the day. I was embarrassed by my honest answer: "I don't know if I actually drank anything other than the pop I had with my lunch." Heat stroke and dehydration (with a touch of stupidity) was my diagnosis.

You know you need to bring your sunblock on your tropical vacation or to the beach; but, if you don't use it, you can't really complain about the fact that you got sunburned or worse. To be honest, that's what we often do. We make a bad choice or think we know best and end up suffering more than necessary. Then we complain about the pain of our self-inflected struggles.

Oh boy, did I ever complain about my self-inflected pain. I actually couldn't wear clothes for about a week. I wore my mom's night gown, and she had to regularly bathe my skin in vinegar water so my skin wouldn't scar or blister. I was burnt so badly it hurt just to stand and walk. (When I had to go to the bathroom, I would literally cry when I had to sit on the toilet.) Mom would even have to get strict with me and force me to get up and walk. The doctor had warned me that if I didn't get up and move, my joints would seize up making it even harder to walk later. I would keep telling her, "No, it's too painful. Don't make me do it!" Yes, that teenage experience taught me a lot about self-inflicted pain! And, more specifically, the importance of not just *knowing* the instructions but also *following them!*

Maximize our Journey

Just like knowing what to expect can help you in the natural, this concept can also be applied to our spiritual lives. And while I have already covered the cycle of grief as a reminder of that process, I feel that showing you some things you might face in your spiritual journey will help you avoid some unnecessary frustration. Perhaps even help you make sense of what is happening right now in your life.

It was November 2018, and I just received the papers that confirmed Going Farther was officially a non-profit organization. Wow, how did I even get here? Many times I wanted to quit because I felt it was just too hard. But my friend Jeremiah, who is an effectiveness coach with the PAOC Alberta and Northwest Territories District, would be right there providing the right resources or encouragement I needed to keep going. But here I was: the founder of an organization! This was my birthday month, so I had a lot to celebrate but still plenty to do.

The morning after this exiting news, I began my morning routine as I always do. I was up really early and spending time with God. I am not a coffee drinker, but let's just say, He is what gets me up in the morning and keeps me going. When I was praying, I felt He didn't want me to turn on my computer to work that day, but rather to just "be." I began to "barter" with Him over a few items on my list that I felt really needed my attention. However, I *knew*, "no work" meant "no work." So, I heard my instructions and I went about my day. Well, that was 4:30 a.m.; but by 9:30 a.m., what was I doing? That's right! I was at my computer working on the task that I was bartering with God over earlier. I would like to tell you that I was being productive and that the day was going by so smoothly, but it was quite the opposite.

Let me begin with the fact that after 2 hours of working on a 1/2 hour task, I could not understand why this was taking so long. Why was this being that difficult? In my frustration, I even started to pray for God to help me. And I think there were a few tears. By this time, my groceries order was ready for pickup. So, I thought I would go, grab my order, and then have my lunch—perfect timing. Off I went.

When I called to let them know I was parked and ready for my order pickup, they said, "I am sorry but your order is not on the list." "What do you mean my order is not on the list?" This was not my first time doing this, and I *knew* I placed the order. But what I hadn't done before was mess up on the "pickup day." While I knew it was not uncommon for me to make a mistake, I pleaded with the lady to see if maybe she could just retrieve my chicken and salad? Normally I would have just pulled my wheelchair out of the car and gone in to get the few items I needed. However, I had not brought my wheelchair with me! I had left it parked in the garage which I sometimes do when I just want to zip out and grab something quick.

Well, the gal heard the desperation in my voice and took pity on me and said, "You know what, I'll go and pull your order. It's a slow day, but I won't get it filled for a few hours." I was delighted by that and thought, "No problem. I'll get a dive through meal for my lunch and have the chicken for my dinner." So back home I went and ate my lunch at the computer.

I know what you must be thinking by now, "Why didn't I just take the day away from the computer as God had instructed?" Well I'll get to that. But let me just keep going. Later I went back to the store to pickup my order around 4:30 p.m. Of course, as you guessed, I was no further ahead with the task I had been working so hard on. But I assure you, that didn't stop me from trying.

Would you believe me if I told you it was 7:30 p.m. before I was finally driving home with my chicken, salad, and all the other groceries? While I won't tell you all that transpired with my order, what I will tell you is the follow-up conversation I had with God while I waited in that parking lot. There I was sitting in the parking lot frustrated and drained from all the waiting. Now I was *really* hungry because it was way past the dinner hour. I started to talk out loud to God, "Okay, what's the deal with today?" I didn't even have words. I just sat there and cried.

As the tears flowed down my cheeks, I felt God speak into my heart. He reminded me of the first time I went to West Edmonton Mall. When I first moved to Edmonton I remember one of the first things I wanted to do was visit the amazing attractions there. I had heard how big and amazing it was, but I had not yet experienced it. I went with a friend and we literally spent the whole day seeing all the sights and doing a little shopping, of course. We were there before the doors opened and stayed until we heard the announcement of the mall closing.

Now it is a true pleasure when I get to take people there to see all the sights for the first time and see their reactions to an indoor wave pool, the sea lions show, a giant pirate ship, or an ice skating rink right there in the mall. It's exciting to point out all the neat things to see. As you're going along among the amazing attractions, you are frequently telling them, "We need to stop and look here at the Ice Palace" or "You don't want to miss the sea lions."

It took me a little while into hearing His unusual reminder before I realized what God was wanting to tell me. On the morning after such a great ministry victory, He was pausing with me to enjoy the wonder of it, but I had just insisted on running ahead. No, He didn't want to show me the sea lions, but He *did* want me to stop, acknowledge my success, and not dismiss it. He had just helped me through yet another big hurdle and this was, indeed, a big accomplishment. Yet, here I was just zooming by it, without a second glance. And I didn't even realize I was doing it.

He said, "Vahen, I don't want you to keep running ahead without appreciating the beauty of what I am doing for you. When I tell you to stop and take time in my Presence, or simply just rest and enjoy where you are, trust Me. There is a reason." Then He went on to say, *"You know how a parent knows when a toddler needs to nap even before the child does? Well trust Me to know that I know when you need to stop or just sit, much better than you do. It's not even about doing or not doing something. I need you to be so in tune with My voice, that you listen and obey all the instructions I give you. Be assured, I know what's best even when you can't see or understand."*

That was the most profound moment for me. And while I haven't always been perfect in the obedience department, you can be sure it's moments like that which help me trust the One giving the instructions. These moments confirm that I should have listened. I *knew* what I was being asked to do, but I deliberately made the opposite choice. *Knowing is only half the battle*.

From my account of that "wasted but not worthless" day, I'm reminded that He can use even the pain of our poor choices to make us stronger and more reliant on Him. This is something that today I definitely understand more than ever. We can learn from our mistakes!

As I've shared before, "Life doesn't get easier or more forgiving, we get stronger and more resilient."[1] But when we learn to follow the instructions that are given, we will definitely avoid some unnecessary struggles. God tells us in Ecclesiastes 4:6, *"One hand full of rest is better than two fists full of labor and striving after wind."* (NASB) And, boy, ain't that the truth! My hope is that this will help you in your current situation and along your continued life journey.

The tools in my survival guide include both *how to prepare* and the *instructions needed* to maximize the journey. I trust that as you continue to read, you'll have a better understanding of where you are and what to expect. And, even more importantly, you'll be guided to see your role in the success of the journey ahead. If I can help even one person avoid one sunburn or unnecessary struggle, then it is most definitely worth it. But I am sure you agree that when trying to prepare for anything, *knowing is only half the battle.*

---

1 Dr. Steve Maraboli, *Life, the Truth, and Being Free,* (CreateSpace Independent Publishing Platform, 2014)

Chapter 7

Who Told You That?

One of my biggest questions I've asked in my Christian walk has been: "Is that You, God?" I don't know about you, but I have doubted God's voice so much in my life that I even wonder how I made it this far. I have questioned the Lord's instructions to me. I have doubted God's voice or questioned my ability to perform something He asked of me more times than I can count. Can you relate? Then, when I *did* start hearing and knowing His voice, the fear of man or fear springing from my insecurities would destroy my confidence and limit my ability to be obedient. Yes, our inability to trust God's voice will limit our ability to obey to Him. In the last chapter I told you about an incident in which I was clearly disobedient and failed to follow His clear instructions. In pondering that incident, I have wondered why I chose that response. My conclusion is: *we don't obey what or who you don't trust, or feel worthy of.* And while it seemed harmless (though I wouldn't have admitted it then), the truth is: I didn't trust that God would help me with what I needed. I continued in my own strength, *because I thought I knew better.* And well, we all know where that got me.

Do you know what I have come to understand? God is much more

---

1 Abigail Pond McKenna, *Too Much Noise,* Image credit

willing to speak to us than we are willing to listen and obey. Mark Batterson said, "Let me make a bold statement and say, learning to hear the voice of God is the solution to a thousand problems."[2] I would like to add: "Learning to hear and *being willing to obey the voice of God* is the solution to a thousand problems." I think it's interesting, that I felt to add "obey" to Mark's quote about hearing, when the original Hebrew word for hear is *shama*[3] as in Deuteronomy 6:4. The definition is very meaningful: "to hear intelligently (often with implication of attention, obedience, etc.). Did you note that it contains *the implication of attention and obedience*! I won't get into a word study now, but it is my prayer that what I share will help you not only be confident in hearing His voice, but also have the courage to obey and to keep pushing forward.

So, just to repeat: if you don't truly know someone, you don't trust them. If we don't trust them, then we most definitely won't walk with them or obey their instructions." And this applies to our relationship with God, too. If we don't truly know God, the trauma of our lives can cause us to have some serious trust issues with Him.

As I look back over my relationship with God, even after I accepted help from Him, I also had to learn to listen and obey in faith. I know that's scary, but again, if we don't trust our guide, we won't be obedient with things that don't make sense to us. When I was being led to my table in that pitch-black restaurant, it was frightening. But I had to trust that my server knew what he was doing and that I was going to be okay.

From my story you recall that I did make my way back to placing Christ at the centre of my life after being derailed by all the trauma. As I became aware that I was hearing His voice again, there was still a definite struggle *accepting* what I was hearing. Simply believing God when He would say," I love you," "You are forgiven," or "I have great plans for you," "You are worthy" was such a challenge. Accepting what He said was like trying to slay a giant I never thought I would see fall. Especially since I was just in the beginning stages of rebuilding my life and I wasn't truly convinced that change was

---

2 Mark Batterson, *Whisper, How to Hear God's Voice, The Loudest Voice in Your Head*, YouVersion devotional, Day 1
3 Shamà, Strong's Hebrew Lexicon, H8085

actually possible for me.

I remember sitting in my kitchen and being overwhelmed with fear. The voices in my head were repeating, "You'll never be able to stay faithful to Vaughan. You're not worthy of this *blessed* life that you are believing for. Who do you think you are?" Well, something inside me just yelled back, "NO! That's a lie!" I said, "I am a child of God and I am loved and forgiven, and God *does* have a plan for me!" I would often yell those words back to the devil and dismiss the enemy's lies: "When I was sleeping around and being a terrible human, you told me how beautiful and amazing I was. But *now* that I am trying to *live right*, you're trying to make me believe that I am worthless and unlovable?" That was the first time I ever yelled out, "You can take your lies and go to hell!"

Why do we continue to believe lies about ourselves or about the One who wants only the best for us? We question and scrutinize everything else, yet we are quick to allow the enemy to lie to us. We walk around defeated and feeling worthless because we are believing lies about ourselves. Perhaps we lack *relationship* with the Lord who is the ultimate voice of truth and enables us to trust and truly believe. But stick around because if you're ready, I am going to attempt to help you understand how to trust in God's truth.

The Voice of Truth

Drawing from the famous speech by Martin Luther King, "Do you have a dream, or something that you are passionate about?" If you were to write one sentence that expresses that dream, what would it be? I am aware that you might not have ever considered the idea of having dreams. Maybe you have been so severely beaten down or traumatized that you don't even know how to dream or feel worthy of a dream. But that is exactly what I want to ignite or perhaps reignite in your heart. Before I tell you my experience, I want you to know that your passions and dreams are sometimes birthed out of much pain or dissatisfaction with a situation. I have a friend who was sexually abused her whole childhood. Her journey to healing was a long and grueling process. However, she has turned that trauma into a powerful passion and is living her dream of helping other young victims. As a result, she is the founder of an organization that helps provide a safe haven for kids who are victims of child sexual abuse. You may know of her: Glori Meldrum. She runs the "Be Brave Ranch" for all the little warriors she is helping. Glori would be the first to say that she was blessed with this journey so she can now help thousands of other little warriors "be brave."

While I had a passion to inspire others from a young age, my passion and dream were even more realized from reflecting back on that season of my life where I was living without peace and joy, struggling to find hope. My personal mission statement is: "To see people overflowing with unexplainable peace, defiant joy, and contagious courage, so they can live in total freedom with unshakable faith, thriving in their God-given purpose." Your dream and passion will be uniquely yours whether you're called to speak, sing, play a sport, be a mom, or simply desire to be happy. Whether your focus is to make a difference in the business community, in the faith community, or your own heart or family - whatever it is, that's what I want you to really focus on for a moment. What do you desire now more than ever?

Can you remember the first time that passion started to be evident in your life? And if today is the first time you even considered a dream or passion would you allow yourself some time to sit and to do just that. And if you do have a dream but it's been dormant, I would like for you to also sit and remember. Maybe your dream seems like an unattainable goal. Can you at least sit and see if you can remember when you *knew* you were born for this? Let me share my experiences to see if will help spark a memory for you.

I wasn't very old before I knew I loved to play with dolls. I would line every doll or stuffed animal (actually anything with eyes and ears) all around my room. I would then just walk in front of them talking and waving my hands. I always wondered about that and concluded that I was born to be a mom. But as I reflected, I realized I wasn't nurturing them or holding them; I was always talking to them.

Another defining moment for me was when I was about 5 years old. I wanted to be baptized in water to take that next step in my relationship with the Lord. My parents were not really sure I was truly old enough to understand what I was agreeing to do, and tried to discourage me. Not that they didn't want that for me, but they just wanted to be sure I understood what I was doing. The day came and we were all standing at a beach in this small town in Newfoundland Labrador. It was a rainy day, so my mom suggested that I wait for another time; but I was determined. Then my dad said, "Vahen, everyone who will go through the waters today has to speak into the microphone in front of everyone and say why they want to do this." Without hesitation I said, "Take me to the microphone."

I knew there was *something* driving me. I couldn't explain it at 5, but I didn't question it. Nor did I have *any* doubts! I listened to that voice inside me and nothing was going to stop me. I heard and obeyed.

As I look back over my life experiences, I can see the early indicators of my life's passion.

No matter where you are in your journey with the Lord (whether you are just starting out, are farther along, or not even ready to publicly acknowledge Him) my guess is that you have experienced some form of communication from Him. A friend of mine was sitting in her car late at night and she just "had this feeling" that she should lock her door. And literally, the next thing she knew there was a stranger banging on her window attempting to get into her car. Times like that illustrate that even when you can't explain it, your choice to follow the instruction proves very beneficial later. At any point along our journey, we can be assured of His desire to share His heart with us. The question is whether we will dismiss it by saying, "That's not God; it's only me."

For those who have that personal relationship with the Lord, John 10:3-4 speaks to us of recognizing His voice: *"The gatekeeper opens the gate for him, and the sheep listen to his voice. He calls his own sheep by name and leads them out. When he has brought out all his own, he goes on ahead of them, and his sheep follow him because they know his voice." (NIV)* The Lord describes Himself as the trusted Shepherd whose voice can be known and safely followed by those who are His own. If that's true, then why do we struggle so much? From my experience, it is because we are believing the *inaccurate* information we are constantly bombarded with. How much better to build a *relationship* with the One we can trust and who is committed to us!

I was in the last stage of writing my first book when I was in training to become a life coach. My coach asked me this question. "Are there any fears or barriers holding you back from fulfilling your dream?" I told her that while I was terrified, I wasn't letting it stop me. She continued by asking me what I was afraid of. I said, "I am terrified that people will judge me when they hear my story. Or that I will ruin my marriage that I have worked so hard to rebuild." I even told her about the nightmares I had about me ruining our marriage. In those nightmares I acted out and declared that I didn't love Vaughan anymore. These dreams were so real that I would often wake up crying. I would have to take a few moments to realize it was just a dream and that I *was* okay.

After I shared that with her, she said, "So you are writing your book, but you're terrified. Tell me what you believe to be the worst-case scenario for when your book is released?" I told her that I was afraid that I would be called horrible names in an interview. If that happened, then I feared that so many painful past hurts in our marriage would come up and would ruin the healing that Vaughan and I had already experienced. Her response to that was: "So what if someone *did* confront you, how would you respond to them?" I answered her, "I would say that I am not that same person anymore."

Then it hit me: if someone wants to believe that or judge me for my past, I don't have to care. That's not who I am anymore! When that dawned on me, I began to laugh! For the first time I understood that *God's truth about me matters more than the opinions of others*. No longer could that fear hold me back. The understanding that God's truth was my confidence lifted a weight off me. (I don't know about you but I'm having a big déjà vu moment as I have had to literally do the same—again! Maybe not the same fear, but I did push through fears of what others would think in order to bring you this book: *Contagious Courage*.)

In order to be free of shame and guilt and live out my dreams, I had to *choose to listen* to the voice of truth plus be obedient to believe what He told me.

Consider the Source

Who is telling you something different than what you know to be true? Who told you that you have to live life in a state of overwhelming fear? Who told you that you're unworthy of love? Who told you that you have to carry shame? Who told you that you are not enough? I realized I was living with way more fear than I needed to. My faulty mindset was, "Isn't it normal to be frightened out of your mind when you start living your dream?" God wants to remove that mindset from me so His courage can flow through me.

I can't help but go back to the first lie in the Bible: Adam and Eve. Their story begins with living in such contentment and in total harmony with the Lord. Then the serpent enters the landscape.

*The serpent was the shrewdest of all the wild animals the Lord God had made. One day he asked the woman, "Did God really say you must not eat the fruit from any of the trees in the garden?" "Of course, we may eat fruit from the trees in the garden," the woman replied. "It's only the fruit from the tree in the middle of the garden that we are not allowed to eat. God said, 'You must not eat it or even touch it; if you do, you will die.'" "You won't die!" the serpent replied to the woman. "God knows that your eyes will be opened as soon as you eat it, and you will be like God, knowing both good and evil." The woman was convinced. So she took some of the fruit and ate it. Then she gave some to her husband, who was with her, and he ate it, too. At that moment their eyes were opened, and they suddenly felt shame at their nakedness. So they sewed fig leaves together to cover themselves. When the cool evening breezes were blowing, the man and his wife heard the Lord God walking about in the garden. So they hid from the Lord God among the trees. Then the Lord God called to the man, "Where are you?" He replied, "I heard you walking in the garden, so I hid. I was afraid because I was naked." **"Who told you that you were naked?"** the Lord God asked. "Have you eaten from the tree whose fruit I commanded you not to eat?" The man replied,*

*"It was the woman you gave me who gave me the fruit, and I ate it.
Genesis 3:1-12 (NLT - my bold emphasis added)*

We must always consider the *source* of the information before we believe it. That was the step that Adam and Eve missed. Then, they tried to blame someone else for their actions. But the choice to act was ultimately each of theirs. When you believe the lies over the voice of truth, you will always struggle with the courage to follow your dreams. And you'll look for any excuse to stay in the prison of your comfort zone.

Whether you have a mission statement for your life or not, the real struggle comes when you actually start to walk it out. Or maybe the struggle for you is the mere thought of considering a dream. That is when you will start hearing the lies. "You will never make it, so don't even try." "You're not good enough." Or "Who do you think you are?" If you hear a voice telling you anything other than what the voice of truth has spoken to you, question it! Consider the source.

Galatians 1:8 says, *"Even if we, or an angel from heaven, preach any other gospel to you than what we have preached to you, let him be accursed."* *(NKJV)* If you are making those first steps toward your freedom, or if you are farther along and trying to make a difference, understand that the enemy *will* attack your courage. If you are perhaps just beginning to use your voice to declare God's truth, understand that the enemy *will* attempt to make you believe the lie that you are not enough. He'll try and make you believe that you are not smart enough or not eloquent enough to speak. Furthermore, if we are not believing the voice of truth, it will affect how you approach God in your prayer life. Believing the lies rather than the voice of truth will affect your ability to choose courage and fight past your fears.

Break the Limitations of Intimidation

Without a doubt, God has called us to be strong and courageous. Therefore, don't be surprised when that courage comes under attack. It's one thing to have the fear of God as we step out. That is a healthy and empowering fear. Like Moses said in his fear of God, *"If you don't personally go with us, don't make us leave this place." Exodus 33:13 (NLT)* However, the fear of man or lack of trust in God to give us what we need are chains that will limit us and hold us back time and time again.

Even in the season of writing *Contagious Courage,* as I have already shared, there have been times of overwhelming fear and intimidation. The phrase "You're not enough" combined with the lie "What can one person do?" threatened to hold me back. The attacks and fears are still very real. However, more than ever before I have come to see these lies and intimidation tactics as actual validation that I am on the right track to fulfill my dream of helping others find freedom.

One morning as I was (yet again) praying through some fear and intimidation, I was reminded of that scene from the movie, "Pretty Woman." Okay, yes, it's about a prostitute and starring Richard Gere and Julia Roberts. There is a scene in the movie after Richard asks Julia to stay with him for the duration of his stay in town. To my surprise, that scene contains the words that really helped me that day; and I hope it helps you. Richard wants to take Julia to some events, but clearly, she does not *look* like someone who can be seen in public on the arm of a wealthy businessman. So, Richard hands Julia his credit card and tells her to go down to Rodeo Drive and buy *anything* she wants, and then he then leaves for the day.

Richard returns only to find Julia back at the hotel in tears and wearing the same clothes as when he left. When he asked her what was wrong, she said, "No one would sell me anything. They said I didn't belong there."

He stands to his feet and says, "Come with me." They go back to Rodeo Drive and Richard insists that the salespeople spoil her and help her look and feel like a princess. When Julia was totally transformed, she returns to the store where the sales lady told her that she didn't belong. With her hands full of high-ticketed items purchased from another department store, and with no intention of spending money, Julie walks up to the same sales lady. Of course, the lady did not recognize her at first. Julia asks her the question: "So, you work on commission, right?" The lady sheepishly answers, "Yes." At that point Julia lifts up her new bags of clothing and responds, "Big mistake!

Big mistake!" and walks out.

Well, that was epic! And that's the scene I was reminded of that morning when I was feeling intimidated by fear. You don't have to believe the lies that you don't belong or that you're not enough. Rather, once you accept what the Lord says about who you are, you can walk out your true destiny in confidence. Or rather accept that you *have* a destiny.

Are there lies that you are believing about yourself or your situation that are intimidating you or holding you back? Maybe you have believed that lie that you're not worthy of a dream. Or that it's too late for you. I've heard people say, "If you're still breathing, it's not too late."

Allow yourself some time to feel God's love meeting you where you are. Imagine God sitting next to you. Allow His love to displace the pain of the circumstances and inaccurate conclusions that were taking up space in your heart.

Julia had possession of that "no limit" credit card but was to paralyzed to access the funds. She had accepted the opinions of others as her identity. When we know "*who* we are" and "*Whose* we are" we won't be intimidated or limited by the opinions of others. When we know that our identity is found in our Heavenly Father, we will know how to access the unlimited resources and unlimited strength that are available to us.

Let's review what we've covered (and discovered) in this chapter: Are you are experiencing some of that fear and intimidation today? Maybe you're stepping out in ways you never have before, yet the lies about who you are or who you can be, are limiting your ability to access the strength and power that is available to you. Maybe for the first time you are considering the notion that courage and freedom *are* for you. Walk out your dreams and passions with confidence in "*Whose* you are" or simply accept the idea you are worthy. And when the enemy comes to tell you something other than what you know to be true, you can walk right up to him and say, "BIG MISTAKE!" "BIG MISTAKE!"

Chapter 8

What's Stopping You?

I trust by now that you're starting to view *you* differently. Or, at least you are starting to see that change *is* possible and that you can be hopeful of a courageous future of freedom as you see the strength that is available to you.

Long before I was an author my father in law asked me a very weighted question. He said, "Vahen, if you could do anything or be anything, and money was no object and there were no barriers in your way, what would it be?" I told him that I wanted to make an impact on the world. I wanted to travel and share my story to encourage others to have courage. But then he replied, "What's stopping you?" I don't think I had ever been more annoyed yet more intrigued by someone as I was in that moment. How dare he imply that *I* was holding *myself* back.

What was I going to do—just leave my job? Who really gets to live out their dreams anyway? It's expensive to travel, and I can't afford that lifestyle. Like someone is actually going to pay me to speak! Besides, traveling is hard on me physically and there are too many challenges. It took me three months to recover physically from our trip to Africa. (To get a window into that incredible experience, if you haven't already, you can read about it in my first book, *Going Father*.) Living out my dream seemed impossible. Plus, isn't that something only people with lots of time and money can do? Just as I said before, how dare he imply that I was holding myself back!

While I was annoyed, it definitely got me thinking. This question turned out to be life-changing for me. So, I'm going to also ask you the same question with the hope that it has the same affect: "If money were no object and you had no barriers, what would you do?" Or, more simply put, *"What's stopping you?"*

You're not going to be held accountable nor are you going to be laughed at for *shooting for the moon.* This is a safe place, so write it down and *dream big.* Then beside your dream, write out what's stopping you from pursuing that dream. Simply stating "I can't" is not an acceptable answer; write out the *why.* As you have also read, believing lies can also form a barrier. I have asked this question many times and have gotten many different responses. However, I don't know which is more disheartening: giving up on your dreams or not dreaming big enough. Maybe you're thinking, "I just want peace!" But is the barrier to that peace conflict at work or at home? Maybe it's financial? Maybe your barrier to your courage and freedom is a past experience or trauma. Maybe you've suffered loss or someone has wronged you, and it has left you with a jaded view of God. Or maybe you simply don't believe that there's anything good in your future.

What's in your way? What's stopping you? Whatever it is, take a few minutes to write it out. If these obstacles weren't in your way, what would you do? If you are already living out your dreams, congratulations. I want you to write out what you are dreaming for *next*? Maybe you need the courage to keep going because your dream is bigger than you even imagined and you need the strength to carry it. You never want to stop dreaming or going farther. But you can be sure you'll need to keep growing your strength and courage. If you are living your dreams, you will agree with me that it's definitely not "easy street."

I have included a diagram with my answers from when I first started stepping out. I trust it will help you write yours. For the record, I haven't always documented everything. I spoke at a conference one time and they had a whole session on "documentation." They said, "If it isn't written down, it doesn't exist." I've totally come to understand that to be true in my life. If I don't write it down in the hours surrounding the event, there is no way I'll be able to remember the emotions of it one year later or even after a week the way I would in the moment. Some of the key elements of my first book would not have been accurately shared with you if I didn't journal it. I understand that sometimes we are just not ready to reflect on our feelings. But, even writing that statement "I'm not ready" will help you when you *are* ready for that next step toward healing.

My Big Dream	My Current Reality/Barrier
I want my story to inspire others and empower them to have courage.	Why would I write a book? First of all, I'm not smart enough to write a book. Plus, who wants to hear what I have to say? Not to mention, I am afraid people will judge me.
I want to exercise and work out because it makes me feel good, and it would be nice walk again.	Why am I working out or trying to walk again? I'm too old to be learning to walk, plus it seems I'm always starting over, and it's frustrating, so why try?
Your Big Dream	**Your Current Reality/Barrier**

As I have shared, many times in the pursuit of my dream I was overwhelmed with fear and insecurities. And, as you may recall, some of my biggest barriers existed when I didn't realize there even was a barrier!

I Thought I Was Free!

One of my favorite times of the year is January. Okay, minus the snow and 30-below temperatures. However, looking past that, I really anticipate the ONE CONFERENCE here in Edmonton. Every year I put a lot of thought into which sessions I will attend. Sometimes it's easy. Like when you know Kay Arthur, Philip Yancey, or Lisa Bevere will be coming. Of course, I select those sessions. However, other times I look at the topics that are aligned with the season of life I am in. But each year I always choose sessions that encourage or challenge me.

So, in 2017 when I saw a FREEDOM session[1] offered at the conference, I was like woo-hoo! This will be a great session for me! I can go and feel proud of the fact that I am free. I might even feel inclined to give myself a pat on the back. You see, I felt pretty good about where I was. I had conquered much in my life already and was just about to step into my dreams with the release of my first book. This was in the same year I was also being trained to be a life coach. And while I knew I didn't have it all together, I was confident in the fact that I felt *free*!

So, the day came and I rolled into the overcrowded room. I was surprised that so many had selected it. My first thought was, "Wow, this is a hot topic." But, at the risk of sounding like a show-off, I told myself I would not comment or share that I felt confident in my freedom.

The session began with the presenter asking us about things that we have in our lives that might be a barrier between us and God. I had already beaten some big strongholds in my life. And, while I knew I wasn't perfect, I didn't think I had anything. He started listing off things like pornography, stealing, and the list went on and on including all sorts of addictions. I was like, nope, nope, I'm good there; no problem there. Until he said that thing that I didn't know was a *'thing:'* "People-pleasing." What about people-pleasing? It was like this big shock to my system. You mean this would be something as damaging in my life as *pornography*? I immediately thought, "I don't know what he's going to say to help me here, but I'm all ears."

---

1 Freedom Session: https://freedomsession.com/ (Online 2021, January)

After he listed off a bunch of the "barriers" he went on to ask us, "So when was the last time you did that thing? (in my case: *people-pleasing*.) I thought, "Oh dear, that was *just today*." He continued by asking, "Why did you feel the need to do that thing? And how did you feel after you did that *thing*?" With his probing, I reviewed the setting in which I had reverted to people-pleasing. Perhaps I had chosen to do it because I wanted to keep the peace. Or, perhaps I wasn't strong enough to say how I really felt. Whatever the cause, I felt disappointed in myself. Disappointed that I didn't have the courage to stand up for myself or tell how I was really feeling. I guess I had concluded that *their* feelings were more important than mine. But to be honest, I was just a coward and I was afraid to speak up or set my boundaries. I was fooling myself into thinking I was doing the *right thing.*

At this point my heart was racing and I thought, "Okay. I have this issue that I didn't even know was a barrier between me and God. Now he's just exposed it. *Ouch*!"

Then he said, "Okay, now that you have remembered the *last time* you did it, close your eyes and try and remember the *first time* you did it." My immediate response was, "Great! He's probably going to get us to look into our childhood; but I'm convinced this isn't going to work for me. Because, you see, I had a great childhood." However, I thought, "What do I have to lose." So, I closed my eyes and almost instantly I remembered a situation when I was in about grade 5. I remembered the teacher asked everyone to bring cookies for a bake sale they were having. Immediately I remembered hearing the voice of another classmate who said with a sarcastic tone, "Vahen can't bring any cookies because she'll burn them before she gets them to school." And everyone laughed. My most popular nick name was "bonfire head."

You see, my red hair and freckles were not as admired then as they are now. I continually was made fun of and called names. If you read my opening lines of *Going Farther,* I said; "Red hair and freckles and a personality to match, I was that little girl who loved being the center of attention. Good or bad attention it was all the same in my young mind."[2] So, as that memory

---

2 Vahen King, *Going Farther – Experience the Power of God That Turns Tragedy into Triumph,* (VKM Publishing 2016), 1.

surfaced, I thought, "See, I told you this wouldn't work for me. Even if you ask my mother, she would tell you that not once did I come home crying or telling my parents any of these stories."

By the time the session had ended, I can tell you I was leaving a *whole* different way than the way I came. I went from being confident to being confused and definitely not feeling free. Should I be worried that this never bothered me as a kid? Should I be crying? And because I'm *not*, does that mean there's something wrong with me? What am I to do? Do I just carry on to my next session? I felt like I was on the operating table having open heart surgery, but the doctor decided to leave. I didn't know how to put myself back together.

Thankfully, the instructor was available for questions, so I was able to approach him. I shared what I had experienced in his session just as I have shared with you. He proceeded to ask me a few more questions. "So, when the kids were saying those things to you, how did you respond? Were you angry?" "No," I replied. "What about shy or withdrawn?" I laughed and said, "Definitely not that." Then he said, "Did you become the class clown?" Well, I wish you could have seen my face. My jaw hit the floor and something went right through my heart. I responded, "Yes, that was totally me. But I thought that laughing about it meant that I was handling it just fine." He said, "Vahen, the moment you didn't speak up for yourself for something that was not right was the moment you started enabling bad behavior and not being able to set healthy boundaries for yourself. That's the point when you started to become a codependent people-pleaser."

I had begun that day thinking I was totally free with nothing to hide. But this freedom session was like a mirror that gave me a glimpse into my soul of another hidden blockage. I could now see that I was held by chains I didn't know existed. But more importantly, was I strong enough to break them? Last time I felt this much uncertainty about my own strength was when I started walking out of infidelity. I'll be honest and tell you, *that* was *easier!*

I feel the need to stop and just acknowledge the title of my book again. *"Contagious Courage."* The path to freedom is a path of harsh realities and tough choices. The chains of our past hold us back from a couragous future. In order to be free, one must have the courage to leave those chains behind. The words of the presenter at the Freedom Session that day literally uncovered a chain I didn't know was holding me back. This is why I'm asking you to journal the story of the mountain you climb; your words could be in someone else's survival guide.

Before moving on, I would like you to reflect on the question that I was asked in that Freedom Session to determine how free *you* are. Is there anything in your life right now that is a barrier between you and your relationship with God? Maybe you're reading this and you don't have that relationship with God and it's okay. But, whatever your spiritual status, would you search your heart and see if there is anything that you have put between yourself and God? And can you acknowledge when you first realized it was there and why it's there? I would venture a guess that the root of it goes back to "people" and how you have been affected by something you have experienced like I had been.

If you would like to take that first step to begin your relationship with God, or simply to have someone to pray with you, I would like to refer you to the Appendix section at the back of the book, there you can find the Crossroads 24/7 prayer line along with some other valuable resources to help in your journey to freedom.

That freedom-releasing incident at the conference session certainly set me on a new pathway of correction. With this new awareness of the bondage of "people-pleasing" I have evaluated *other* major moments in my life where I forfeited my freedom with the best of intentions! Or, where I had made my choices out of fear of man and not in obedience to God. I am so thankful that the Lord has equipped me to catch the tendency so it won't hold me back. And as a result, I am experiencing much more freedom and authenticity in relationships. Yes, it is still a challenge to set boundaries and let go of what people think of me, but I will tell you it no longer paralyzes me with fear.

20/20 Vision

Barriers are all around us, both seen and unseen. Even now, as I write these chapters, I am smack dab in the middle of yet another "unseen" barrier. Another one that I was not even aware of. (I guess that's why it's so appropriately named "unseen.") But this barrier is not to *my* freedom, but to *someone else's*. This barrier is one of the most heartbreaking of all the barriers I have encountered. It goes deeper than I can begin to uncover in our short time together. However, I would be remiss if I didn't acknowledge it. I have had to sit and spend time confessing this and asking for forgiveness. What is it, you ask? I have consistently had a lack of understanding of what people of colour or the Indigenous people have suffered and are still suffering as a result of "my" silence. The sad realization is that generations have stood by and remained silent or uninformed. Our silence has blocked millions of people for generations from experiencing *true* freedom.

While it's something I am now aware of, I do realize that it's something that may not easily be forgiven by those we've wronged. (I am so thankful for the *Lord's* forgiveness as I have repented and brought this before Him with a broken heart.)

It's interesting to me that I've lived so long with this ignorance. Yes, I could certainly speak from experience about the stereotyping of people in wheelchairs. But this fresh awareness of how both my lack of understanding and my silence against prejudice and injustice endured by people of colour, has resulted in another "unseen" barrier being brought out into the light. Despite the magnitude of the need for change, our responses really are an individual heart issue. In her book, *So You Want to Talk About Race?* Ijeoma Oluo said, "Once you start to see yourself, you can't pretend anymore."[3]

I have begun to take responsibility for my own heart and I pray that you are doing the same. I can see now that my own ignorance in past relationships has caused others to suffer. However, now that I am aware of these barriers, I have started educating myself, asking questions, and doing my part to *be the change.* Loving people where they are and for *who they are* is something

---

3 Ijeoma Oluo, *So You Want to Talk About Race?*, (Seal Press 2019), 4.

I've determined in my heart to do. Who's with me?

There is so much more I can say here. While I can't even begin to understand the depth of it all, I do know that my part is simply to love. With that said, maybe you can write out what you feel about the issue of racism in our society and how we can together "be the change" that this world needs. Grappling with these issues in the past months has certainly been part of arriving at "20/20 Vision" and seeing my world much more accurately.

Freedom will not merely come from a few reflection notes, but we must start with "seeing" the blockages and then have the courage to walk it out. "If we continue to treat racism like it is a giant monster that is chasing us, we will be forever running,"[4] say's Ijeoma Oluo. I want to also echo that with the message I am trying to share as the central theme to this book, *Contagious Courage.* If we treat our own fear and bondage like these giants that will never fall, we will be forever running.

Affirming Discoveries

Before we move on, allow me to leave you with one more nugget. Around the same time my father-in-law asked me: "If you could do anything and there were no barriers, what would you do?" He also asked me: "How would your life and character be different if you fulfilled your dream? In April 2014, this was what I wrote in my journal:

"I would hope that my character would reflect that of Christ, so I would want to start now. That means I would definitely need to spend more time in prayer. And my life would look different, in that I would need to be careful of distractions and stay focused on being a master at time management. I would need to be a good steward of my time. If I was living my dream, I would hope that my passion would be contagious and that I would inspire others to want to change."

About 4 years after writing those words, I began a segment on my YouTube Channel called *Contagious Courage.* Since then I have interviewed

4 Ibid., 7.

some amazing people with incredible stories of courage each month. My intention was that these stories would empower others to choose courage. Can you imagine my shock when I found my journal entry with those powerful words years after it was written. I had no recollection that I had written it, but these words were still relevant and still definitely a part of *my* survival guide.

I understand the value of these words today more than ever. These journal notes continue to provide great insight and confirmation along my life journey. It's why I continue to encourage you to also write down your thoughts and goals in your own journal.

Remember, one major barrier that could be stopping us from moving forward into our dreams is our self-perception. How we view ourselves really can shape our development. I have embraced the personal motto: *"Confidently Imperfect"*. It allows me to accept my mistakes without guilt and focus on improving next time around. Even now, there are times when I am being introduced or when I get feedback from something I have written or spoken, that I say: "Wow, are they really talking about me? Am I *actually* living my dream to encourage others with *my* courage?" I want you to know that every time I hear something like that, my confidently imperfect self declares that my trust and faith is in a big God. He is able to do way more than I could ever hope or imagine. My confidence is in Him and that's what people see: *His* strength, through my weakness. And yes, I would say that's pretty amazing. Honestly, with His strength, I feel "unstoppable." I believe that when you reevaluate your perspective on courage, you will also begin to reevaluate your perspective of your *role* in it all.

So... What's Stopping You?

Your answer to this probing question will shape both your expectation and even your motivation. And trust me, writing it *now* will help you down the road. Habakkuk 2:2 advises us from scripture to *"Write the vision; make it plain on tablets, so he may run who reads it." (ESV)* I believe this is a perfect example of what we need to have in place to keep going. Your written vision for your life is like a road map, and yes, even a survival guide. If you don't have one, you won't know where you are going. You'll end up wandering with no purpose or direction. This is a good place to pause and reflect, because there's still lots of "walking in the dark" up ahead that I'll be challenging you to embrace.

I pray that as I share more of my discoveries of how I was able to find this contagious courage and unlock a level of freedom I didn't know existed, it will help you in your journey to see freedom is within your grasp. And so, with all due respect, I'll ask, *"What's stopping you?"*

Section 3

Courage To Grow

Truth Be Told

Lie number one you're supposed to have it all together
And when they ask how you're doing
Just smile and tell them, "Never better"
Lie number 2 everybody's life is perfect except yours
So keep your messes and your wounds
And your secrets safe with you behind closed doors

Truth be told, The truth is rarely told, now

I say I'm fine, yeah I'm fine oh I'm fine, hey I'm fine but I'm not
I'm broken
And when it's out of control I say it's under control but it's not
And you know it
I don't know why it's so hard to admit it
When being honest is the only way to fix it
There's no failure, no fall
There's no sin you don't already know
So let the truth be told

There's a sign on the door, says, "Come as you are" but I doubt it
'Cause if we lived like it was true, every Sunday morning pew would
be crowded
But didn't you say the church should look more like a hospital
A safe place for the sick, the sinner and the scarred and the
prodigals like me

Well truth be told, The truth is rarely told...[1]

1 Matthew West / Andrew Pruis, Truth Be Told lyrics © Highly Combustible Music, Two Story House Music, One77 Songs, Musixmatch 2019

Chapter 9

Win The Day

What if I told you that I bought a gym membership last January, would you be impressed? Maybe not; everyone buys a gym membership in January. Like many others, when I see those commercials with people and their well-toned, fit bodies, it *really* motivates me to hit the gym. Now what if I told you that I go every day without missing once; would that impress you? Okay, now I have your attention. I've got my routine perfected: I sit at the edge of this busy gym and watch everyone work hard, sweat, and get fit—I even cheer some of them on!

You're probably saying out loud, "Vahen, that's absurd. You can't get fit that way. You're just wasting your membership!" Of course, you're right. Attendance and motivation alone are not enough. We actually need to do the work in order to grow.

I was sharing my struggles about my exercising and eating habits with my sister and we both acknowledged that the struggle is very real to be healthy. We agreed that we definitely needed a new plan. So, we gave each other full rights to get in each other's *business*, if you know what I mean. I even created a private Facebook group called, "We Actually *Love* Working Out." In this space we would tell each other when we were working out and what we were eating. We even gave ourselves permission to fail and not beat ourselves up if there were days when we just couldn't do *the right thing*. I am embarrassed to tell you how long we lasted. The daily struggles of life and lack of discipline would constantly interfere with our desire to do better. I finally reached the point of saying, "What's the point?"

Yes, I have fallen off and then climbed back on that wagon more times than I care to admit. But I am still getting up and back on. While I have a long way to go, I am happy to say that I have been back on the wagon with *some* consistency with my eating habits and working out. I am actually back doing physiotherapy again. I am focused on winning each day. I call it stumbling forward.

Stumbling Forward

I had the privilege of interviewing Mat Embry, a documentary filmmaker. After receiving a diagnosis of multiple sclerosis, he set out on a journey to find the best treatment to manage his own health. Mat is a trailblazer and strong advocate for change in the world of treatment for MS patients. One thing Mat said in that interview that really stuck with me was this, "There are no cheat days!" What do you mean, no cheat days? Everyone has cheat days! The first time I heard Mat say that in a social media post prior to our interview, I jokingly dismissed it. My response: "Everyone has cheat days." Right? But, as I interviewed Mat, the same words spoke volumes to me. He said, "Just think about it. If you have one cheat day a week, that works out to roughly 15% of your life. So, if you want to be at 100% health, how do you expect to get there when you are only trying about 85% of the time?"

I wish I was disciplined enough with my diet and exercise to even say "my cheat *day*." However, if I am honest, for far too long *every* day was a cheat day for my physical health. So, when I heard *"no cheat days"* all I saw was a giant that I will never see fall in my life. And while I was trying, I knew it was not enough. Too often I ended up at the same place. As I said in my introduction, if you're not moving forward, you'll eventually go backwards.

In 2016, I progressed to 11 unassisted steps and was able to walk the block with my walker in 20 minutes. Fast forward to 2020: before returning to physiotherapy I could maybe make one or two unassisted steps on a *good* day. And, walking outside with my walker: impossible! I could barely make it to my kitchen and back without being winded.

Laughing and dismissing the no-cheat-day rule doesn't seem so funny to me now. And, do you want to know something ironic? After talking with

Mat, I realized that I actually hold to the no-cheat-day principle spiritually. This required something of me. The struggle was indeed real! I had to fight to sustain the "no cheat days" in my relationship with the Lord. I don't take a break from His Presence. God gets me *every day*! And 99% of the time He gets the *first* of my day.

Have I always had that view? Not even close. Looking back, I was on and off the wagon more times than I can count. I would live on experiences and emotions until my feelings got the better of me. Then I would find myself running to God only when I *really* needed Him. Sometimes in my frustration I would just conclude, "What's the point?"

Growing spiritually isn't much different than improving physically. It's easy to apply that same faulty thinking of expecting instant results to our spiritual growth. We want to be spiritually strong. We even look at others who we would love to be like, but we want it *now*! Rarely do we want to wait or accept the work required to grow. The motivation that we get on Sunday or from an inspirational podcast is great, but we actually need to spend time every day with God and actively put into practice what we learn in order to grow spiritually.

I received this message from someone who read my first book. They said, *"I finished your book. Although I'm sure it was not your intent, it pretty much convicted me that I've all but given up on the ministry work I set out to do. Not because I want to give up, but, because I feel I've gone in so many wrong directions trying to find what God has for me. I also get jealous of people who say they have heard God speak to them, as I never have, despite praying and asking Him for guidance.*

I want His direction in this, but I am not one to sit around waiting. So, when the answers don't come, I'm substituting my own or doing what others I respect feel I should be doing. Did I mention that I'm impatient?"

In all the times that I have had to start over physically, what if I had just quit? What if I had continued to beat myself up for what I didn't do or failed at? I wouldn't be able to get back up. Like I have heard Mat say, *"You just have to win the day."* That is the same for you and your relationship with God. You just have to win today! So be intentional to spend time with Him today. He will always give you what you need for *this* day. And what you receive from Him will have a positive impact on your *next* day. Keep in mind, however, that what you receive from Him might not be the answer you were wanting or expecting. But you have to trust that God desires only the best for you.

Recommitting my life to Christ and asking Him to heal the broken parts of me were sign posts along my journey, but growing stronger and going farther in my relationship with Him daily? Well, that required a whole other level of surrender and discipline that initially I was *not* prepared for.

I can totally relate to Paul when he said, *"I don't really understand myself, for I want to do what is right, but I don't do it. Instead, I do what I hate" Romans 7:15 (NLT)*. When I read this verse, I think about all the things that we could possibly struggle with like drug addiction, pornography, emotional eating, people-pleasing, or any number of things. I have come to see how relevant this scripture is when applied to maintaining discipline in other areas of my life.

Discipline to exercise and eat right or the discipline to maintain my relationship with the Lord all seem to fit the *struggle* of this scripture! What I want to do, I don't do, and what I don't want to do, I do! Yes, that has been illustrated in my life more than I've even been bold enough to share—until now.

Giant Slayer in Training

While you might not think that skipping one or two days with God will matter in your overall spiritual health, consider the parallel in the natural disciplines. You might feel you can get away with choosing a bag of chips to replace a meal rather than taking the time to make a proper one. It may be assumed that such a compromise will be without consequence. But, it *is* a big deal for your overall physical health, especially if that once-in-a while turns into *often*.

If you are training to be an athlete or preparing to climb Mt. Everest, the training you must subject yourself to trickles into every area of your life.

You need to be physically and emotionally strong in order to go farther or, at times, even to survive. You're probably thinking, "I'm not training to be an athlete or climbing Mt. Everest." But, this is also true with your spiritual muscles. Don't eliminate yourself from higher levels of training. Spiritually, you are training for something bigger: your ongoing freedom!

"This is why change can be so difficult. Change is always emotional. You have to decide, very intentionally, who you are going to be every single day. If you don't make the decision who you will be and how you will act, then your body will go through its cycle seeking the same chemicals and emotional states that it has become accustomed to. If you don't start your day with intention, you are living in survival mode. Your time is, without question, moving faster than you want it to. You're stuck in the past. You're stuck living out the same experiences and emotions and patterns, over and over and over.[1]

Our courage and freedom do not automatically happen as a result of just one big choice that we make. Rather, it's about finding the courage to be strong enough to conquer all the little ones along the way. Just like how the little compromises in our everyday thinking can limit us from reaching our full potential and full freedom, little courageous choices we make to adjust our thinking will set us free with limitless potential.

Now back to my current journey. I have just shared with you how I've struggled with my exercise, eating habits, and walking. Well, I have a praise report. As of September 2020, I am actually back to making unassisted steps again. Can I get a "Woot, woot!" As I write this I am super excited. I started *"doing the work"* and while it was only small, baby steps, I *am* seeing improvements. I am up to 7 unassisted steps; and, who knows where I will be when you read this? Regarding my eating, do I always say "no" to eating that cupcake or the jujubes I want? No, but I *am* making better choices for my overall health. While my new patterns of self-discipline are still *in process*, I am making progress! Therefore, I give you permission to ask me after you read this how my health is. Ouch! That made me a little uncomfortable, but I am open to making myself accountable. And that is what I am asking of you:

---

1 This Morning Routine Will Make You Unstoppable, Benjamin Hardy, PhD
   https://medium.com/thrive-global (Online 2021, January)

intentional effort and accountability. Keep trying! Win the day!

Additional Tools

As you consider ways to get back up or to "win the day," I want to introduce you to a visual tool called a "Balance Wheel." It's simply your life at a glance. Lets' begin by looking at my chart. I have chosen and written in six areas that are important to me or ones I would like to improve on. I continue by giving each area a number from 1-10 on how well I am doing in each area. "1" means I'm in desperate need of help. "10" means I'm good and I don't think it could possibly get any better. However, I always hesitate giving a "10," because I feel there is always room for improvement. Then for further evaluation, I answer two probing questions in relation to my current situation.

My Balance Wheel

Here's the example of my own chart with the areas I've selected and how I rate my level of satisfaction for each. I include it here, along with some additional tips for goal-setting, to help you see how valuable this exercise can be in helping you move forward. The times I have acknowledged *where* I am, or *how* I am in a particular area and set goals to improve have been when I have experienced the most success.

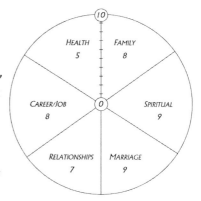

I gave my marriage and spiritual life a "9." And, from what you have just read of my life, you have seen why I am so excited to be able to celebrate a 9. Yes, there is always room for improvement, but I have learned to acknowledge what is going well and be proud of it because it is important to celebrate your success.

My weakest is my health. I gave myself a "5" in the health department and I have chosen to illustrate it further here since it is the area that for me, needs the most improvement. And as you've just read, it's my biggest struggle. I also want you to see here that your weakest area is also the area that you can experience your greatest rewards. Let me illustrate, by sharing a few comments regarding my physical health.

What's going well?

I am alive and independent when the doctors didn't even think I would live, never mind be able to care for myself or accomplish all that I have. While I am not where I want to be with walking and maintaining overall good physical health, I'm not were I was. I am learning discipline, doing what I can, and not beating myself up for not doing what I can't.

What's not going well?

In this area, I am easily discouraged and often tempted to quit. That is why I fall off the wagon so often. Yes and even eat a bag of chips as my meal replacement. Therefore, if I am not careful it can affect me not only physically but emotionally and spiritually as well. Then this leaves me feeling bad because I "just can't."

Goal-setting Tips

For me it's about planning the different things I need to do the night before. Like planning when I will do that 15 minutes of strengthening exercises. And yes, even scheduling the times I am to stop and actually eat. However, what is also important in the initial steps is understanding that there may be days you "just can't." For example I have experienced this when I am traveling or when I know my body is exhausted. Sometimes there are random days when you "just can't." You will need to have grace for yourself on those days. This is why small attainable goals are so important. This might not sound like a whole lot to you, but doing something small constantly *will* build discipline. And that **discipline** *will* build confidence. And, you'll start to add more to your routine. Let me just pause here: saying "I can't" with regard to knowing your limits is much different than saying "I can"t just because you are holding yourself back out of fear.

Another important tip when setting goals is to not compare yourself to other people's goals. If I asked you how many steps you did today and you said 10,000 steps, do you think it would be realistic for me to get discouraged because I only did 11? Man, if I did 11 unassisted steps every day, you can be sure you'd see this girl celebrating! Or if I compare myself to Mat and his "no cheat day" disciplined routine, I will miss celebrating the days I actually ate my meals and did my workout for the day.

I used to fixate on all the things I couldn't do. I would get so overwhelmed and say, "What's the point?" And I would quit. So when I was successful in doing 5 minutes of "something" everyday, I thought to myself, "What else can I do?" And because of that mindset, I was able to walk and make unassisted steps.

If I would have listened to the doctors' prognosis and quit then, I would not be where I am today. Even with all the times I have fallen off the wagon and had to "get back up," can you imagine the excitement I will feel when I can give this area a "9?" And, the excitement I will feel when I *am* healthier and making *even more* unassisted steps: indescribable!

Now, it's your turn.

Getting started: THE EMPTY BALANCE WHEEL

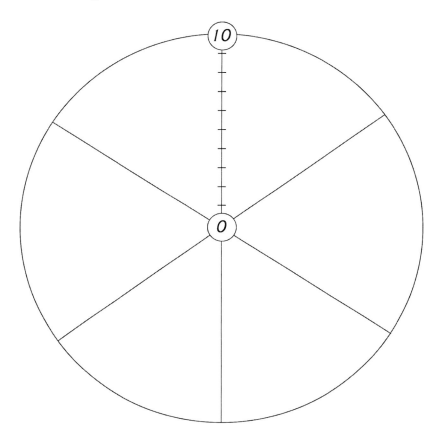

Let's start your self assessment. Consider the possible areas you wish to assess and fill in your own chart. • Family • Career •Spiritual • Physical Health • Mental Health • Education •Financial • Recreation and leisure •Relationships (You can even break this down further: marriage, spouse, sister, mother, friend, or co-workers.)

Continue by giving each area a number from 1-10 on how well you are doing in each area. "1" means I'm in desperate need of help. "10" means I'm good and I don't think it could possibly get any better. Congratulations if you scored a "10" on any area. However, like I said, I always hesitate giving a "10," because I feel there is always room for improvement.

Next write down one thing that's going well and one thing that is not going well or you wish to change or improve in each of these areas. After you have done that, write one small attainable goal for each area. My recommendation for the goal-setting part would be to focus on only one area at a time and to set small, attainable goals. This will be key for sustainable growth. But devoting time to each now will mean you will have that momentum available when you are ready to add more to your routine.

What's going well? What's not going well?

1. Was there anything that didn't go well today that you can let go of to help you in starting better tomorrow?

_____

_____

_____

_____

2. What one thing can you do today that will help you win the day?

_____

_____

_____

_____

I challenge you to look at all the areas that you are weakest in. And rather than condemn yourself or resenting these areas, think about the overwhelming blessings you can receive from them if you're willing to work at it. At one point, my marriage and my relationship with God were both between "0-1." Now they are my strongest and have brought me the most joy. From reading my story, I am sure you now understand why I can celebrate with such passion. I have learned to manage this area with the mindset to "win the day," and "do what I *can* and God will do the rest." I do not beat myself up for what I can't do. This mindset has really helped me to keep moving forward. I am hoping that it will encourage you to do the same. So, start out small. Don't be too hard on yourself and reward yourself for your accomplishments! You are already in motion to *"win the day."*

Chapter 10

Grow Through What You Go Through

When I first started sharing the story of what Vaughan and I went through as a couple, I would often get a response like, "You're so brave. Weren't you afraid to share these struggles with the world?" Following this was the awkward moment where they would sometimes feel inclined to say, "I don't judge you." Other times I would have people get annoyed with me when I would tell them that I am confident I'll never be unfaithful or lose my faith in God again. Some wonder how I could make such a claim. I would tell them: "It's not that I am invincible. It's just that I am grounded enough in my relationship with God to have the confidence *in Him* to say that I never have to go back to that life again." How awful it would be to live my life in fear and to not know the joy of true freedom from the chains of my past. That would be classified as merely surviving and I want to thrive.

Two things I started to see early on were: if you have never known true freedom, you can't understand true freedom, especially when it comes to the "big stuff." The other thing I started to see was that if I was constantly worried about whether or not someone judged me for the bad choices of my past, it would really limit the freedom I could be experiencing now and into the future. I started saying, "I am glad that you don't judge me; but, if you did, that would be *your* burden to carry, *not* mine." Can you imagine if every day I said, "Boy, am I glad I made it through today without sleeping around?" I will tell you that initially that is *exactly* how I felt, but that is not freedom. However, once I *was* free, I wanted to tell everyone. Not because I wanted to air my dirty laundry, but because I knew I had overcome that battle, and that if I could be free, others could also.

If we know that we are prone to fall back into old patterns and that our spiritual growth is a slow process that requires a lot of work, wouldn't it make sense that God would want to help us? He wants us to be grounded in Him and have deep roots so we can withstand the pressures of life and walk in freedom. But how is it possible? How do you develop deep roots?

Let me begin with telling you *where* the roots grow. And you probably already know this, but roots grow in the heart. Luke 6:45 says that *"A good person produces good things from the treasury of a good heart, and an evil person produces evil things from the treasury of an evil heart."* (*NLT*) What you say (and do) flows from what is in your heart.

Jesus tells us a parable in Luke 8 about our heart being the soil and the word of God being the seed. He said,

> *A farmer went out to plant his seed. As he scattered it across his field, some seed fell on a **footpath**, where it was stepped on, and the birds ate it. Other seed fell among **rocks**. It began to grow, but the plant soon wilted and died for lack of moisture. Other seed fell among **thorns** that grew up with it and choked out the tender plants. Still other seed fell on **fertile** soil. This seed grew and produced a crop that was a hundred times as much as had been planted!*
> *Luke 8:5-8 (NIV - bold emphasis mine)*

He goes on to explain these different soil types and how the condition of our hearts will determine how we respond to God's word.

Footpath - The seeds that fell on the footpath represent those who hear the message, only to have the devil come and take it away from their hearts. This prevents them from believing and being saved.

Rocky Soil - The seeds on the rocky soil represent those who hear the message and receive it with joy. But since they don't have deep roots, they believe for a while, then they fall away when they face temptation.

Thorns - The seeds that fell among the thorns represent those who hear the message, but all too quickly the message is crowded out by the cares and riches and pleasures of this life. And so they never grow into maturity.

Good Soil - And the seeds that fell on the good (fertile) soil represent honest, good-hearted people who hear God's word, cling to it, and patiently produce a huge harvest. Vs 12-15 (*NLT*)

For me, my heart's default mode resembled the seed that fell on rocky ground. Yes, I would get excited about the message and accept it. I would believe for a little while, but as soon as life got hard, I gave up because I didn't have deep roots.

When I accepted Christ's help during that major time of rebuilding my life and relationships, that's actually when He began to work on my heart. I learned that if we aren't continuing to guard our hearts from all the thorns choking us, the good seed won't be able to take root. God's desire is to cultivate the soil of our hearts so His seeds will grow and multiply through us. As we surrender to His Presence within us, His Spirit produces His fruit of love, joy, peace, patience, kindness, goodness, faithfulness, gentleness or meekness, self-control... See Galatians 5:22-23 (*NLT*)

Did you catch how we grow? With surrender and patience! Even though it's tough, keep trusting and keep waiting because the seeds *are* growing. I have allowed bad seeds of insecurities, self-doubt, fear, bitterness, and pride, (the list goes on) to take root in my life for far too long. I've blamed others for my pain and let seeds of unforgiveness grow even deeper roots, which caused even more pain for me and those around me.

Even now, I have to be careful because where faith, hope, and love are blooming, I am still at risk of sowing seeds of doubt, faithlessness, or unforgiveness in my heart. You see, no matter how beautiful your garden is, there is always a risk of weeds growing and overpowering your beautiful garden. And all of you with a "green thumb" understand that. You just learn to dig those weeds out before they choke out the good things that are growing. Again, I feel the need to say, *"Above all else protect your heart, for everything you do flows from it." Proverbs 4:23 (NIV)*

Right Environment For Growth

Have you ever witnessed the delight of a toddler learning to walk? Do you get upset if they don't get it right the first time or even the fifth time? No! My guess is that you're grinning from ear to ear and loving the beauty of the process. You're probably even laughing with them and loudly cheering them on, not caring that you look or sound funny doing it. "Awe! Look! Oh almost! Oh! Oh! You got it! You got it!"

The ideal growing environments are the ones where it is a safe place to fail. Some of the best teachers I've had in school or in any training were those who said, "This is a safe place to fail." They understood the intimidation that comes with learning or trying something new. Am I ever glad that God has exactly this environment for you and me to grow in. Don't be afraid to fail or fall, get back up and try again!

Sometimes we are placed into environments that push us to grow that may seem anything *but* good at the time, from our perspective. Before my first book was launched, I remember asking God to remove me from a toxic work environment. I wanted to be "out there" doing ministry. I started praying, "God, I'll go anywhere, just get me out of here." Many times I wanted to quit my job. However, the Lord's reply was consistent and clear: "Vahen, this *is* your ministry. When it's time to go, I'll let you know."

Don't let me mislead you. I played my role in that toxic environment. I contributed to the office gossip; my character was not what it should have been. Learning to say nothing was my toughest challenge! I learned that in my effort to defend myself, I was disparaging someone else! Even when I was speaking up because I thought it was "helping the cause," I was only adding to the tangled web that I never should have been caught up in. I had to learn when it was time to speak or when it wasn't. Those were vital opportunities to learn dynamics that would help me in the next season of my life as a leader.

Embrace Discomfort & Be Willing to Wait

It really is a life-long process to learn to wait for the Lord's timing. I remember being introduced to this in my first living away from home experience. It was my first year in college and I remember sitting on the steps watching my parents drive away. I was just sobbing. The only life I knew was small-town Newfoundland Labrador. And here I was in a big city so far away from the comforts of home. It was terrifying. My friend's dad, who was also a pastor, saw me crying and came over and sat beside me. He said, "Vahen, in your walk with God and in your future ministry, there will be many moments where you will feel stretched like an elastic band. When you think you can't stretch any more, God will take you farther. Stay close to Him and He will sustain you. You will grow stronger in Him, but He will not let you to break." Little did I know how powerfully that message would play out in my life!

This was advice that I have often looked back on. Although it didn't make the painful growth experiences any more bearable, it *did* help comfort me knowing I was not alone in feeling stretched.

Just knowing that you will have many unwelcomed pauses of waiting along your spiritual journey will be most beneficial. The more you embrace the process, the "easier" it will be. Okay, maybe not *easier*; but when you embrace God's strength and guidance in that process, *you* get stronger. Whether it's bad soil, unsafe environments, or impatience, there are always things that will threaten to destroy the good seeds that have *already* started taking root.

Allow me to share from a devotional that I read when I was in another one of my painful, stretching and waiting times. *Divine Guidance* was actually the title. It began with this Bible verse, *"God is working in you, giving you the strength and desire to do what pleases Him." Philippians 2:13 (NLT)* The author acknowledged that phrase *"working in you"* and went on to say:

> God does this as you engage your mind, open your mouth, move
> your feet, and use your hands to do what's He's already put in
> your heart to do. The moment you say yes to God and to His will,

He gives you the ability to perform it. Notice, He doesn't reveal
His will to you and then call you. He calls you, and as you step
out in faith and obey Him, He reveals His will to you step by step,
empowering and equipping you as you go. If you're thinking you'd
like a little more detail before you make a commitment, take note.
God may make you uncomfortable where you are.

Like an eagle that stirs up its nest...to teach her children to fly, a
mother eagle literally pushes them out of the nest. Talk about
being out of your element! Can you imagine what they are
thinking? "It's my mother doing this to me." But until a baby eagle
is forced out of its comfort zone, it doesn't realize it was born to
fly, spread its wings, release its power, and take its place in the
heavens.[1]

Our uncomfortable situations are the unwanted yet precious ways God will use to prepare our hearts and to grow deep roots. Yes, I had said, "Lord, here am I. Send me. I'll go *anywhere*!" But I had to learn to wait as Psalms 27:14 says, *"Wait patiently for the Lord. Be brave and courageous. Yes, wait patiently for the Lord." (NLT)*

While I was working in that toxic work environment, I finally accepted and was ultimately *willing* to embrace the discomfort of the *waiting* process. I decided to start to write my first book during that time, and then shortly after that He said, *"Go!"* and I was laid off from that job. Then I was able to finish my book. If I had quit as I had begged God to allow me to do, I wouldn't have grown in patience and self control or gained more understanding of love and forgiveness. I also learned the beauty of what God does in a situation when we are willing to let Him. I wouldn't have been able to receive unemployment insurance as income in the transition before my book tour if I refused to wait for the Lord's timing. And the best part of waiting was gaining the new relationships that were developed as a result of "hanging in there." I had the best send-off from my workplace that I could ever have asked for. I received a "journal" with the inscription, *"Just a girl who decided*

---

1 Jentezen Franklin, *Divine Guidance, The Word For Today,* https://jentezenfranklin.org/daily-devotions/divine-guidance-2-2?cid=sm-fb (Online 2021, January)

to go for it" and a card with more precious words of affirmation and support than I felt worthy of.

Remember the "Hope Conference" I told you I was involved in planning and coordinating? No one really knew just how insecure I was going into that day. This was my first big event and no one realized how challenged I felt because of the responsibility of managing all the details of the day. I was so aware of how important this day was and I wanted to do a good job. How empowering it was to have words of encouragement spoken to me that day just when I needed them in order to feel confident in the task. I remember one moment as I was speaking some negative words over myself and Jesse (my co-emcee) said, "Vahen, you're a natural host, just be yourself. You're doing great." His words really encouraged me in the midst of this "bigger than me" day. Having people who create that safe place around you as you're figuring it out is priceless.

Yes, I really appreciate having a safe place in my growing times. However, what I have learned to value even more is the grace to grow in an environment that may not feel comfortable or safe. And, while we're learning to embrace the waiting in that uncomfortable place, we should treat ourselves and others with grace.

Enlarging Our Capacity

When you're growing, you may feel like you're being stretched beyond your capacity. And at times, you may experience more emotions than you feel you can handle. You may even feel "out of your element" and extremely uncomfortable. But when God is stretching you, He is actually enlarging your capacity plus your roots are growing deep. You can trust the Lord. He won't fail you. Trust and grace are vital elements as you are growing. It's absolutely true: *we grow through what we go through.*

If growing is never easy and predictably uncomfortable, how then can one prepare and even cooperate with God for increased growth? Let's review the steps we've already covered. First of all, don't resist the *process.* We won't be able to grow without it.

Secondly, if we continue giving God only our quick or hollow prayers which are mixed with but a *little* obedience while expecting our confusion, pain, or stress to subside, we will continue to get uprooted. *John 15:5 tells us that "I am the vine; you are the branches. If you remain in me and I in you, you will bear much fruit; apart from me you can do nothing." (NIV)*

Thirdly, make that fresh surrender of your will to the Lord. Allow Him to be the Master of your destiny each day. For many years my heart was hard and I was unable to grow anything good. But, when I surrendered my will to His, He was able to transform me. He dug out all the anger, bitterness, pride, and need for control that was cemented in my heart. Only then were my roots able to go down deep allowing room for the fruit of love, joy, and peace that is contagious to grow.

Fourthly, are you placing more value on relief from the pressure of your situation rather than on the potential to benefit from it? Are you simply begging God to just remove you from your difficulties? Or, are you willing to wait until He says it's time? Would you like to see how God can turn your pain situation into something amazing?

You don't have to like all the things you might go through, but I pray that you'll be brave enough to ask God to change *you* and allow Him to help you handle the situation.

I want you to see that it is more than just being willing to stay and *endure* a situation. The key is to embrace God's strength, so you are truly able to *grow through what you go through.*

Chapter 11

What Does Your Fruit Taste Like?

With great humility...

I humbly and publicly confess...

the biggest struggle in my life as a Christian is...

being right about everything, all the time

Comic Title: False Christian Humility

SearchingforGrace.com © Mick Mooney

Have you ever bought fresh fruit from the grocery store and then take a big bite anticipating some juicy goodness? But, with that bite comes the sad realization that your *fresh* fruit isn't so *fresh-tasting* after all? Disappointing, isn't it? I think it's interesting that in the scriptures, our lives and how we are to live are compared to fruit. Psalm 34: 8 says, "Taste and see that the Lord is good..." *(NIV)* How can others taste and see that He is good? You guessed it. By *our* fruit.

You might still be smiling at the cartoon I have here. Let me say that when the fruit of our life isn't good, other people will know it. They will leave our presence with a bad taste in their mouth. In the previous chapter I mentioned that we needed to ensure that our hearts are "*good soil*" so our roots can grow deep and produce "good fruit." Fabienne Fredrickson said, "The day you plant the seed is not the day you eat the fruit. Be patient and stay the course."[1]

Ah yes, that painful *growing* process. That process along with the waiting was something I also covered in the previous chapter. What is the expression of good fruit in our lives? How many of you have heard of the

---

1   Fabienne Fredrickson, Quote: https://www.facebook.com/IAmBoldheart/photos/a.71187326231 2300/1119494431550179/?type=3&theater, www.boldheart.com (Online 2021, January)

Fruit of the Spirit? If so, can you list them all? I mentioned a few already, but I'll list them here again. *"But the fruit of the Spirit is love, joy, peace, long-suffering, kindness, goodness, faithfulness, gentleness and self-control..."* *Galatians 5:22-23 (NKJV)*

They sound nice, don't they? But I wonder, have you ever explored the meaning of each of them? Is the fruit of the Spirit evident in your life? While you may or may not be able to answer "yes" to these questions, I do believe we all can tell of a time when we've tasted the bitterness or sweetness of the fruit of someone's life.

Now, here's my question: "What does it look or feel like when God is *preparing* my heart to grow good fruit? The verses in Jeremiah 17:7-9 tells us about both the "good" and the "bad" that can flow out of the heart. *"But blessed are those who trust in the Lord and have made the Lord their hope and confidence. They are like trees planted along a riverbank, with roots that reach deep into the water. Such trees are not bothered by the heat or worried by long months of drought. Their leaves stay green, and they never stop producing fruit. The human heart is the most deceitful of all things, and desperately wicked. Who really knows how bad it is?"* (NLT)

It's only my surrender to the Lord that "prepares my heart" so that He can produce that "good fruit" in me. I cannot produce this fruit in my own strength merely through trained, disciplined behavior.

Here are a few questions to ponder before we begin to look closely at each of the fruit of the Spirit. (Do you have your journal page and pen ready?)

1. Can you remember a time when you left someone's presence with a bad taste in your mouth?

_____

_____

_____

_____

_____

2. What does the fruit found in your life taste like?

_____

_____

_____

_____

_____

3. What can you do today to ensure that the fruit of your life is good to the taste?

_____

_____

_____

_____

_____

A closer look at each of the Fruit of the Spirit will assist us to see ways that we can begin to soften areas of our hearts in order to grow better tasting fruit.

Love

Have you ever said, "God, I want Your love in my heart," but, you were wondering why you have to love *that* person? I would never tell you that you are not a loving person. However, I feel sometimes we are so consumed by our own pain or circumstances that it causes us to hate and not love. Okay, maybe "hate" is too strong a word, but do you *withhold your love*? Maybe you say or do things that you *know* will not help in a situation? Is your need to "be right" or to "make them pay" greater than your desire to show love?

It's unbelievable to me that not once in our journey to a restored marriage did Vaughan *ever* bring up the past or withhold his love to purposely hurt me. I was on the receiving end of love when it didn't make sense. I am so very thankful that Vaughan chose not to act out of his own pain, but instead chose to love. Remember me, that seal caught in the net? His unconditional love set *me* free to love.

In your journey of trying to love someone through their pain, or even in your "everyday of life" are you able to choose selfless love? Or do you make a situation worse by responding from your own pain, insecurities, or need for control? I do realize that in the early stages when we are still healing from past pain and rejection, we may still have the tendency to respond negatively. However, the more we allow God's love into our heart, the softer our heart will become. And, the easier it will be to show His love.

I know there are many different ways we can approach this topic of love and I am merely scratching the surface. However, before moving on, I'd just like to say that some of the same outcomes described regarding forgiveness also apply to love. Loving someone doesn't mean always returning into the same relationship as before. Nor does it mean that loving will happen quickly. It is a process. And as a friendly reminder, you can't *truly* love someone else if you are not *truly* healed or know how to love yourself. But I'll leave you to dive into that more in your own time. Just know that if you hang on to hate or unforgiveness in any area or for any reason, your heart will stay hard. You won't be able to grow good fruit in your life.

Read God's definition of love in 1 Corinthians 13:4-7. *"Love is patient and kind. Love is not jealous or boastful or proud or rude. It does not demand its own way. It is not irritable, and it keeps no record of being wronged. It does not rejoice about injustice but rejoices whenever the truth wins out. Love never gives up, never loses faith, is always hopeful, and endures through every circumstance." (NLT)*

Love is something I must *choose*. I must choose to love others whether I feel like it or not. Furthermore, I've certainly learned that love is essential if there is any chance for the other fruit to grow.

If I could speak all the languages of earth and of angels, but didn't love others, I would only be a noisy gong or a clanging cymbal. If

I had the gift of prophecy, and if I understood all of God's secret plans and possessed all knowledge, and if I had such faith that I could move mountains, but didn't love others, I would be nothing. If I gave everything I have to the poor and even sacrificed my body, I could boast about it; but if I didn't love others, I would have gained nothing. 1 Corinthians 13:1-3 (NLT)

1. Has there been a time when you received selfless love? How did you feel?

_____

_____

_____

_____

_____

2. When God says that if you don't have love it means nothing, how does it make you view areas you are struggling to show love?

_____

_____

_____

_____

_____

Joy

Before I went to Africa back in 2012, I was convinced that God would heal me. You see, the slightest disruption to my eating and bathroom routine would cause me to suffer for days and sometimes weeks without relief. And now I planned to travel to a third world country?

Only days away from my trip, while experiencing another 3-4 hour painful night in the bathroom with no relief in sight, I cried out to God. "Where are you? I know you see me! I know you feel my pain! So why haven't you taken this?" I bargained with Him and said, "If you heal me, I'll travel the world and share about your love and great power." My joy was put to the test.

I went to bed that night dejected and wondering why God didn't care. This was a regular feeling for me. The next morning when I opened my devotional to look for "something," the first words I read were "All My Tears." The scripture from Psalm 56:8 followed: *"You keep track of all my sorrows. You have collected all my tears in your bottle." (NLT)* The devotional went on to say, *"It's a common misconception that if God doesn't rescue us from our pain, it must mean He doesn't care. On the contrary, He is very personal with us, and cares deeply."* While I still didn't understand it, I made the choice to trust Him. I went on my trip believing that if He didn't "take" my pain, then He *would* be with me in it. By faith I chose to believe.

When we arrived at the airport in Uganda, I had another moment when I was having serious doubts about my decision to go there. Although we received an amazing greeting and even though I was so excited to meet the people who would be our hosts for our trip, the emotion of it all was just too much. I actually cried on the way to the host's home.

Soon all of my questioning and doubting seemed to fade. God used the people we went to speak with, also to *speak to me!* From the first day I arrived in Africa I had people tell me they could not understand the joy I had. One pastor actually said, "What is this that I am seeing? This girl is in a wheelchair, but yet she has so much joy." That was just one of the many stories I have where God was using my joy to encourage others when I didn't *feel* it. Was that trip exhausting? One hundred percent. However, it was during that time that I began to grasp the concept of *true* joy. God was showing me that when I serve Him with joy in spite of my pain, people will taste and see that He is good.

I interviewed Philip Yancey for my NIGHT OF COURAGE gala back in November 2020. He said, "Pain redeemed is more impressive than pain removed." And that's what I was I beginning to truly understand during that "God, why aren't you removing this" season. I was growing in joy and allowing

"The joy of the Lord to be my strength." Nehemiah 8:10 (NIV)

Are there any circumstances or people in your life that are making it difficult to experience joy? If so, can you explain why?

_____

_____

_____

_____

Peace

What would you say if I were face to face with you now and asked you, "Do you have peace?" Would you say, "I'll have peace when my bills are paid... when my kids are settled... or when _____?" You fill in the blank. Are you waiting for a situation to turn around before you can experience peace? The sad reality is that the majority of people would say they do not have peace.

Life isn't easy and we all suffer in different ways. In the COVID-19 pandemic there was distress and frustration on a level we had not experienced before and may *still* be experiencing. Maybe you said, "I'll have peace once the pandemic is over." Maybe you think it is impossible to experience peace. Philippians 4:4-7 tells us to *"Rejoice in the Lord always. I will say it again: Rejoice! Let your gentleness be evident to all. The Lord is near. Do not be anxious about anything, but in every situation, by prayer and petition, with thanksgiving, present your requests to God. And the peace of God, which transcends all understanding, will guard your hearts and your minds in Christ Jesus."* (NIV)

In the past, this verse would always make me feel anything but peaceful! In fact, I felt condemned! How would I ever be able to do what it was declaring? This seemed to be yet *another* giant that I would never see fall in my life. If we know that there will always be anxiety and chaos, how can we ever have peace? And how can we possibly rejoice! And ALWAYS?

Do you know who wrote this? A man named Paul, who was being held in a Roman prison. So, if anyone had "just cause" to be anxious, it was Paul. When stressful situations are causing anxiety to rise, the only way I have been able to hold onto peace is to do as Philippians 4:4-7 instructs, by giving it all to God. When I surrender my "not so good circumstances," it releases His power to guard my heart so that I can experience peace. I read a great article once that said, "our goal must be to know Christ in the middle of the conflict. Peace is the fruit of the presence of God's Spirit. This means you can always know peace. We may never eliminate conflict but we can always know the peace that comes from knowing the God of peace."[2]

1. How often do you experience anxiety or restlessness that causes you to lose your peace?

Never---------Seldom---------More than I would like---------Every day

2. Who or what are the common factors when this happens? Are there any boundaries you can put in place that could help you be more peaceful?

_____

_____

_____

_____

_____

Before we continue on, I would like to acknowledge that yellow caution sign again. When you start practicing the expression of these fruits *by faith,* it may be uncomfortable and or even unbearable at times. You may feel like a pushover or someone who doesn't know how to speak up or stand up for themselves. Or maybe that was just me, because "at first" it felt like people- pleasing. But I assure you it most certainly was not. When your focus

---

2 Shepherd Press, *Peace is Not the Absence of Conflict*, https://www.shepherdpress.com/peace-is-not-the-absence-of-conflict-2/ (Online 2021, January)

is shifted from pleasing people to pleasing God, you will be able to view people and your circumstances differently. Which brings me to the next fruit.

Long-suffering

Long-suffering can be defined as "patiently enduring lasting offence or hardship."[3] Each of these words matter. Being patient and enduring lasting offense or hardship? Who wants to grow in that? No one likes waiting or enduring, especially if it's through hard times. It's one thing to wait for an appointment or wait for that call-back about a job. But being confined to a wheelchair for over 20 years or 16 years of being in a prison of the four walls of a bathroom for hours on end—these would definitely give me some education in the "patiently enduring" department. When people tell me I'm being patient, I simply compare it to other things I have endured. And, to be honest, being patient comes easier as a result of the capacity gained to endure "lasting hardships."

There are many situations we could talk about where we don't like waiting for the solution or the conclusion. None of these is fun. There's a familiar verse in Isaiah 40:31 *"But they that wait upon the Lord shall renew their strength…" (KJV)* I knew it was all about sustaining expectation. But, the word "patiently" was intended in the original Hebrew word.[4] I struggled to get my mind (and heart) around that word. But, the Lord is indeed so gracious to give us grace to patiently endure.

And that's why it's so fittingly named long-suffering. I haven't seen anything more accurately describe long-suffering than what I read in a message from a friend. We were actually talking about trusting God and waiting on His timing. She said, "W.A.I.T., is to Willingly – Abide – In – Trust."

I am embarrassed to admit it, but there are some people I have very little patience with. I really have to "dig deep," if you know what I mean? Then there are others in my life who could mess up terribly and I would still

3 Longsuffering: https://www.patheos.com/blogs/christiancrier/2015/08/17/what-does-longsuffering-mean-a-biblical-definition-of-longsuffering/ (Online 2021, January)
4 Qâvâh, Strong's Hebrew Lexicon. H6960

find it easy to lavish them with grace. But with the Lord, because I am in love with Him and I trust Him completely, I will *wait* on Him and *wait for Him.* I am confident that He will never let me down. Plus, if He's "late," as I have often accused Him of being, I have come to understand it's for a *very* good reason. So, I willingly abide in trust.

1. Can you think about a situation when you have endured long-suffering?

_____

_____

_____

_____

_____

2. What have you learned or are still learning from your waiting experience?

_____

_____

_____

_____

_____

Kindness

I represented Canada on the world stage in the Miss Wheelchair World pageant in Poland. I have many stories I could share, but one specific moment really stands out in my memory. That incident illustrates that being generous or kind when you don't have to be (or when it's not expected) goes farther than we may realize.

It was the day before the final gala. We were on the main stage practicing our routine. As we were rehearsing, I saw one of the videos on the big screen from another contestant: Miss Netherlands. She was stunning. However, when her beautiful smile should have been the focus, the bright red lipstick smudged on her front tooth stole the show. I immediately thought, "Oh no! If that were me, I would be horrified." I didn't get time to see the contestant before we left, but I decided to go right to the producers and inform them. I knew that it would only be a quick video edit and it could be fixed. They assured me it would be taken care of. Then we all dispersed for the evening.

The next morning at breakfast I saw Miss Netherlands and told her about it. Her response was surprising to me! She was more taken back by my act of kindness for her than the embarrassment of having the lipstick on her teeth. So, when it was time for the vote for Miss Kindness World, I was told it was unanimous. I was the choice of all my "fellow-sisters."

This quote by Seneca sums it well: "Wherever there is a human being, there is an opportunity for kindness."[5] If we are willing to see it, there will always be opportunities to be kind. Being crowned *Miss Kindness World* was the most surreal experience. But even more incredible was the way God displayed His kindness through me on that world stage. I've never seen anything defuse a situation more quickly or ignite hope so quickly in someone's eyes like an act of kindness. Love expressed by a kind act communicates that indeed the individual is loved and is valued. No wonder the scripture reminds us, *"And be kind to one another..." Ephesians 4:32 (NKJV)*

1. When was the last time you did an act of kindness and you didn't expect anything in return? If so, how did it feel?

_____

_____

_____

_____

_____

5 Seneca philosopher. https://www.quotes.net/quote/8834 (Online 2021, January)

2. Have you ever been on the receiving end of someone's kindness? If so, how did that make you feel?

_____

_____

_____

_____

Goodness

Have you ever wondered what it means to be good? How many times have you heard a parent say the phrase, "Be good to your brother and sister." Or maybe you've heard a co-worker say, "Be good to so and so; it's their first day." I feel the implication here is that I *am putting aside my needs or natural tendencies to treat someone differently.* Sometimes this happens in moments when we least expect the value it will bring to the other person.

Remember that Newfoundland and Labrador trip I told you about when I was away for a month? Well on the trip back home, and on our 3rd delay with two more flights before I would arrive home, there I sat at the Halifax airport—exhausted. The lady sitting next to me rather imposed upon my "misery" by striking up a conversation. She said, "Hello, I am admiring your beautiful wheelchair." Then she continued, "I have had some problems with my feet. But sitting here watching you and your beautiful smile, I feel so guilty, because I often feel self-pity." She talked about some other tragic things she'd been going through. We talked, we cried, we laughed, and I even prayed for her right in the airport. I gave her my card and left (finally!) on that much-delayed flight. Next day I read this note on my YouTube channel. *"I have been blessed to meet Vahen November 11, 2019 at Halifax airport gate 20. This meeting will be forever in my heart.*

I was blessed to see Vahen in her beautiful wheelchair. What a great conversation starter and what a conversation it was. Little did I know at first that I was meeting someone as ordinary, and yet as extraordinary as Vahen.

And Vahen, if you read this, thank you for your words, your time, and your attention. You were an angel that was sent to cross my path. I needed you that morning and you appeared."

Being good isn't always as fun or as easy as being bad but expressing "goodness" is necessary if you want to serve good tasting fruit. That "expressed goodness" benefited both of us that tiring day in the airport.

There is a life principle that my father in law shared with me one time and it has been something that Vaughan and I have tried to live by. That principle has definitely helped me be "good." He said, "Never give or lend anything that you expect to get back." That goes for money, physical items we have, our time, and yes even your words of encouragement. There are many different scenarios in which you can use this principle; however, the real issue is our *misplaced expectations*. What about when we volunteer our time? Or encourage someone and we are not "rewarded" as we had hoped or expected? Are we still able to be good to them? Or do we begin to resent the person and the time spent and complain that we're not valued? Are we able to truly release it? Who are we trying to please and for what reward? If we want to be good, we must learn to give with a pure heart and with the right motives. *"God loves a cheerful giver." 2 Corinthians 9:7 (NIV)* So choose "goodness" and give with a cheerful heart in all areas of your life. Leave the outcomes and rewards to God. Learning this valuable principle will be a process and it may be hard at times.

1. Are there any good works or good deeds that you have done which have left you disappointed because you didn't get what you were expecting in return? Does this experience stop you from doing or being good in other areas?

_____

_____

_____

_____

2. Read Matthew 6:4 *"Give your gifts in private, and your Father, who sees everything, will reward you." (NLT)* **Write down one thing that you will try today that will help you embrace and express goodness in your life.**

_____

_____

_____

_____

_____

Faithfulness

When I first told Vaughan that I didn't know if I was able to remain faithful, it was because I was only relying on my own strength. I genuinely doubted myself. But as I put my trust and faith in God again, He taught me how to be someone who could be trusted. I had someone ask me as I was writing this chapter, "How do you prove to someone you are trustworthy after you have hurt them?" I said, "You simply stop focusing on trying to convince them with your words that you are changed, but focus instead on changing *you.* Your life becomes the evidence of change." Only time reveals the true nature of someone's trustworthiness. I also heard someone say, "The only way you can know if you can trust someone is to trust them."

Are you trustworthy? The fruit of faithfulness applies to all areas of our lives. Would you say something behind your friend's back that you wouldn't want to say to their face? It's embarrassing to admit that you are not a faithful person, isn't it? Trust me that this was a quality I hated in myself and found difficult to change. The truth is that at some point in our lives we have all been unfaithful in some way or another. Being aware of these areas and acknowledging them is a major step forward.

How do we grow in faithfulness? The foundation is really formed by looking afresh at the Lord as the ultimate definition of "faithful." Scripture reveals many examples of His faithfulness. Secondly, we grow in expressing faithfulness as we become more confident of who we are and "Whose" we are. That sends us back to the Word of God! The Spirit reveals those areas where we are tempted to either throw people under the bus (failing them) or to devalue ourselves by not being trustworthy. Once you learn the value of being a faithful person who is trustworthy, it will be worth more to you than money or fame can buy.

1. List some areas where you feel the quality of faithfulness is important.

_____

_____

_____

_____

_____

2. In the areas that you have listed, how faithful are *you in each area*?

_____

_____

_____

_____

_____

Gentleness

Philippians 4:5, tells us, *"Let your gentleness be evident to all." (NIV)* Is your gentleness evident to all? That's a good question. Have you ever held a newborn baby? Chances are that when you were being handed the little bundle of joy, you instinctively knew to be gentle with it. I wish life were that easy. However, while our words or actions that we pass on to others do not come with warning labels, we most definitely need to be gentle. We actually have the power to damage someone's heart.

When we aren't gentle with someone, why do you think that is? Is it because we think they should know better; or, do we simply think we are better than them? Perhaps those seem like harsh words. But whatever the excuse we make for not being gentle, the root cause may well be that we are holding on to pride, anger, or the need for control.

There are many different scenarios I could suggest where expressing gentleness is important. A basic trait that would help us with our gentleness (and a good place to start) is humility.

1. Would you consider yourself to be a gentle person?

_____

_____

_____

2. Are you able to speak and respond with gentleness in situations, or are people left with a bad taste in their mouths because of your bitter fruit?

_____

_____

_____

Self-Control

Have you ever *lost* your self-control? Maybe you said or did something in the heat of the moment and found yourself having to apologize after the fact? Yes, I get it. It's tough and we've all been there. I remember getting my daily intravenous fluids changed when I was in the hospital. Let's just say the nurse was not "gentle" with me. I was feeling like a pin cushion. Finally, I couldn't take it anymore and I blurted out, "Apparently they didn't teach bedside manners in your training, did they?"

Oops! Of course no one is perfect, but the more you are yielding to the Spirit for His fruit of self-control to grow in your heart, the better you will become at *denying yourself*. As we grow in expressing what He is growing in our prepared hearts, we also grow in seeing situations through a different lens. And, while there are areas which are a "safe environment" for growing, quite often you don't have that luxury. But we can always make it our goal to *be* that safe place for others—even under pressure. As you have already heard me say, traveling is hard on me physically. So, the "normal everyday" is not so "normal." This is what I was contending with when I was on one speaking tour. My mother and I were driving to the next location where I was scheduled to speak. We decided to stay overnight at a local Inn. We arrived early, got settled and looked forward to a great meal after a long day of travel.

I remember looking at the menu and wanting *everything*. The selection process was difficult, but I finally decided and placed my order. When the plates of hot stew and fresh dinner rolls were placed in front of me, I didn't even pay attention to how fast I was eating. After a few bites I stopped. Hesitantly I asked my mom if her meal had an odd taste to it. I said, "I can't quite tell what it is, but I know *something* isn't right." It didn't take us long to realize it tasted like mold. Ugh! Mold.

I knew I had to tell the waitress why we had stopped eating our meal, especially after expressing how hungry we were. Even though we had every right to complain, I decided to simply inform her rather than sharply complaining. She apologized profusely and didn't know how this could have happened.

When we finished, we *still* left her a good tip. I knew that I could show God's love by not complaining or making her feel any worse than she already did. Do I always get this right? No. But, after what came next, you can be sure I now always *try*.

I spoke at the event and we continued on. Much to my pleasant surprise, the next day I found this note waiting in my in-box from the owner of the Inn where we had stayed. *"Vahen, it was a pleasure to meet you. You truly are an inspiration. I want to apologize for the meal you had, because this was by no way our standard or what we pride ourselves for. Please come by again on your travels and allow us to treat you properly! Free of charge. I do hope you come back and see us again. In having an awful stay, you were gracious, sweet, kind and forgiving. It was our pleasure, truly, to meet you. God Bless."*

Now there might be some of you saying that I am just a push-over and afraid to speak up because of my people-pleasing tendencies. But I assure you that responding kindly in these settings is much more the heart of God than if I had ranted on about it. I love how we have the opportunity to feed people good fruit, even when we least expect it. Because my heart was soft with love and patience, I was able to offer *good fruit*. What does your fruit taste like?

1. Has there been a time when you have allowed your emotions to control the way you responded in a situation?

_____

_____

_____

_____

_____

_____

2. If so, explain what you were feeling when you lost control. Why do you think you couldn't control yourself in that moment?

_____

_____

_____

_____

_____

_____

3. And lastly, on a scale of 1-10, what does your fruit taste like?

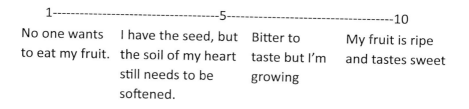

1------------------------------------5------------------------------------10

| No one wants to eat my fruit. | I have the seed, but the soil of my heart still needs to be softened. | Bitter to taste but I'm growing | My fruit is ripe and tastes sweet |

Without a doubt, God is preparing your heart in order grow good fruit. Don't' forget: it doesn't matter how much you say, "Jesus loves you," no one will believe you if the fruit of your life doesn't taste good. As you learn to view yourself and your circumstances differently, it is my prayer that you'll either see Jesus more accurately, or that you will represent Jesus more accurately. Either way, my prayer is that people will taste and see that He *is* good.

I know some people get uncomfortable talking about how Jesus can take your pain or that He gives strength. Maybe it's because you've had a bad experience with bad-tasting fruit. Thus, you have not been properly introduced to the One who can really make the difference. If that is the case, let me say that I am so sorry you've had a bad experience. May I have the privilege to ask you to consider Jesus as an option if you are struggling to find love, joy, or peace in your life. It is my desire for you to *begin* to see Him for who He truly is. He is the One who loves you unconditionally no matter what lies you've believed about yourself, or what others may have said *in Jesus' name.* A little "food for thought" as we journey on.

Section 4

The Cost of Courage

Pursue

Steady my steps as I walk
Through the path that You have set before me
Take what is weak within these bones
Carry what I can't on my own

Your word a lamp to my feet
To the places Your calling me

I pursue You God, I chase after Your promises
I pursue Your heart and the pattern of Your ways
I pursue You, I pursue You

No, I wont be afraid of whats ahead
You're walking with me every single step
Guiding me to the other side
O Jesus my reward and my prize

Oh let Your love, be always guiding me and,
Open my eyes to see the wonder of Your way
And let my life, bring Glory[1]

---

1   Pursue, Brooke Nicholls, © Brooke Nicholls Music (2019).

Chapter 12

What Are you Seeking?

Following the Lord is an amazing thing, but going farther is also demanding. Sometimes it's a lonely road and the stakes are high. In the words of my editor and dear friend, Peggy Kennedy: *"For all of us who know the amazing (yet demanding) privilege of partnering with our God, the stakes are high! Let us allow His Spirit to sharpen our capacity to receive and respond to revelation. He is fine-tuning all of us to receive what the Spirit is revealing. When we hear His voice calling us to come up higher, will we obey? It will be said of us that we have done what He desires, when we embrace His ways above our own."[1]*

I acknowledge that what we have covered in the last three sections has been quite heavy. And now, moving into the final stretch of this book, you will be getting a glimpse of what it costs to cross over from merely surviving to thriving. I am confident that you are seeing what "choices" are essential to maintain a life of freedom with a courage that is contagious.

When I was about 7 years old I received a very important life lesson that rings even louder to me today as an adult. I remember sitting on the front seat at church and being so excited to see the visiting pastor. He was very interesting to listen to. That might have had something to do with the fact that he would often ask questions and sometimes engage the audience by asking for volunteers to illustrate his point. And this time, when he asked for a volunteer, without hesitation I was the first to thrust my arm high in the air. My chubby cheeks and ear-to-ear grin only got bigger when he chose me!

When I went to the front he said, "I have a choice for you. I have two things in my hands, and you get to pick one." He continued, "Here in this

---

1 Peggy Kennedy, *Hear The Sound*, (Newsletter July 1, 2016) http://www.twosilvertrumpets.ca/

hand is a Bible and in my other hand I have a $5 bill. You can have either; the choice is yours."

I don't remember how long it took for me to respond. All I remember thinking was, "$5 is a lot of money for a 7-year-old;" but I choose the Bible. After making my selection, he handed me the Bible and when I opened the front cover, there sat a $5 bill. This scripture was handwritten on the inside of the cover, *"Seek ye first the kingdom of God, and his righteousness; and all these things shall be added unto you." Matthew 6:33 (KJV)* I don't remember anything else about his message, but this life lesson will be forever embedded in my mind.

All my life this verse keeps coming back to me, but not always in a good way. Sometimes I would find fault with the Lord and pray, "But God, I love you. Why aren't you giving me x,y or z? You said if I loved you all these things would be added unto me."

After becoming paralyzed, I remember being in a service where the preacher actually pointed me out and said, "God wants to heal you." Then his next breath was, "Come back Wednesday." (This was Monday.) Well! You can imagine my excitement as I anticipated Wednesday night.

I attended Tuesday, and finally the day came that I had waited for. My healing!

Vaughan and I arrived and sat expectantly through the whole service. As it was coming to a close, I wondered when the pastor was going to address me. After he finished his message we were sitting around following the end of the service. In front of everyone he said, "I am sorry I don't have it." He continued, "All I felt God wanted me to say was, *"Seek ye first the kingdom of God, and his righteousness; and all these things shall be added unto you." Matthew 6:33 (KJV)*. If the pastor said anything else, I don't remember. But I will tell you that hearing that scripture *this* time, did not have the same effect as it did on my 7-year-old self. And I can assure you I did not leave grinning ear-to-ear. I did everything in my power to hold back my emotions. Why did it affect me so negatively? Somehow all I heard was "You're not good enough for God to heal." Maybe those people who told me there was something wrong with me were right and that's why God didn't heal me. I didn't understand. I thought I *was* seeking God. What was I missing?

Some years would pass before I heard a very humorous but convincing response from the Lord in answer to that intense questioning.

I remember when I was shopping with a friend and found this amazing purple patent leather purse. It was stunning. The only thing was, I didn't have any shoes to match. What do you wear with a purple patent leather bag? A pair of purple patent leather shoes, of course! I looked in every store I could think of. This hunt went on for over a week. When I unsuccessfully exhausted the list of all the stores I could physically visit, I took my search on-line. It didn't take long to find the perfect pair. They were stunning and matched my patent leather bag perfectly. I added it to the cart. As I was going to check out and pay, I received a pop-up notification that read. "Unfortunately, this item is no longer available; we apologize for any inconvenience." No! That can't be right! I even called the company, hoping to hear that there was just a glitch in the on-line system. Surely that's all it was and I *could* get my size 7 shoes; and, all would be right in my world.

No such luck. So you'll never guess what I did next? I ordered a half-size smaller. I told myself, "I don't stand in them anyway, so I can squeeze into them and I will be fine." I got them, and I confess that I only wore them once—maybe twice. Vahen! They are not your size! I know, right!

They sat in the box for *two years* as I wallowed in denial. Finally, I knew it was time to acknowledge that they're too small and I needed to part with them. Did I? No! Not right away!

A few years later, when I spoke on this very topic, I actually brought them as part of my illustration. I told my audience pretty much what I told you. At the end of my talk I told them that I was doing a draw for the purple patent leather bag and the shoes (for anyone who was a size 6 1/2.) Yes, the bag, too! Because what would someone wear with purple shoes? Yes, it's okay to laugh or shake your head. I am doing the same as I relive this absurd experience.

But, why have I even shared it? In my life I have sought after many things; but if I am honest, I have not sought after my relationship with God with even half of that intensity.

I was reminded of the time my mom said to my younger self, "Vahen, if you spent half the effort on your insides as you do your outsides, you'd be much better off."

Let's jump now back to the year 2015, when I was asked to help facilitate a lady's prayer meeting. As I was praying for each of the ladies, I won't lie; I felt a little intimidated. I was like, "God, there are so many different needs. What do I pray for each lady?" In response He showed me this beautiful picture of Him standing in front of me. These ladies were coming for healing — whether it was for emotional healing or physical healing. Yes, I was doing the praying, but it was actually Him they were coming to. He was giving each one what was needed.

As I rested in knowing that God was right there with me giving me the words to pray, He also spoke something else into my heart. He said, "Vahen, these prayers of healing are for you as well." I began to weep, because I had pretty much given up on expecting God to do something like that for me. I simply didn't want to be let down again. I even said to Him, "God, I don't care about a healing; just grip my heart because I never want to doubt you again." I was literally just focused on seeking God and *not* the gift that I *thought* I was supposed to get from Him. But in that moment God was showing me that I couldn't be that close to Him and not believe big things from Him. He was telling me afresh that it was okay to ask. And that night as He spoke those words, I felt "something"—not only in my heart, but I felt something physically that I hadn't felt before.

That night when I got home, I used the bathroom "on my own" for the *first* time in 16 years without medication. I was in such shock I was trying to explain it away. I would like to tell you that I embraced it and was so thankful, but unfortunately, I believed the lie that "one time" wasn't a healing. But the funny thing was, "one time" after "no time" in 16 years was indeed a healing! However, I kept this news to myself. I journaled my routine for 3 weeks before I actually believed I was healed! At that point I remember being in the front room working out and I felt God say, "Why don't you believe what I am doing?" With that I felt released to share with my close friends and family. But the sad thing was it was still 3 months before I could stop journaling: "no medication!" "no medication!"

I was so afraid to be let down and to be told that I would have to go back to that prison that I had cried out to God to remove me from so many times. Could I actually believe that now that prison was gone? I no longer had those 4-5 (and sometimes) 8-hour bathroom visits. Wow! — the emotional brain space that it freed up! What was I to do with all this extra time and energy? Oh wait! I know! I now had the energy and strength to actually finish writing my first book, and had the freedom to actually do a book tour. Talk about freedom!

In this chapter we've covered a lot of ground from my childhood lesson of chosing the Bible over a $5 bill, to purple patent leather purses and matching shoes. Yet all of these stories combine to remind us of what seeking Him *first* really means. I have sought after many things in my own strength or desires for many years, and it left me empty and disappointed. But when my focus has been on my relationship with the Lord, He would always *"add unto me."* Reflecting on *my* journey and the message of Matthew 6:33 I hope to remind you to *not* let the *things* that God would add unto us become the *things* that we seek. *What are you seeking?*

Chapter 13

What's Your Muster Point?

Do you have a comfort food? That snack you're drawn to when you need that extra "something." I find it hard to pick just one, but if I had to, it would be jujubes. There was a time when I would literally get Vaughan to put them out of reach before he left for work so my consumption could be "monitored." Okay, you're probably thinking, "Vahen, that's not a comfort food—that's an addiction." And you're right. I have been working on reducing my sugar addiction, but don't even the healthiest people out there have their comfort foods? What's yours? If you had to choose one, what would it be?

Oh, and what about after a long day? What is it that you do to unwind or shut off the brain?

Do you flop on the couch and watch your favorite TV show or movie? Do you sit with your favorite book or a glass of wine? For me, my favorite times are when Vaughan is home and we just drop everything and for a game or movie night. There are times we laugh at the fact that we are sometimes like two teenagers with no parents in the house. We're eating whatever we want, doing whatever we want and when we want to. It's great!

We all need comfort food and self-care plans in place. But what happens when what we use to unwind or relax becomes *a place of escape.* You might be thinking: "What's the difference? Or the harm?" Let me explain.

It was the summer of 2019 and I was taking a day away to turn off the brain if you will. While I was sitting having lunch, I saw a sign: *muster point!*

We all know what a muster point is, right? *A designated place to run to in case of emergency.* For the rest of that day, the phrase *"Where do you run to?"* kept replaying in my mind.

I thought about when I was diagnosed with transverse myelitis and my life got turned upside down. I lost my independence, my self-worth, and my identity. I gradually started removing God from the center of my life. I started running to people and things for the emotional fulfillment that I needed. Yet all this was only leaving me feeling even more empty and alone! God was not my muster point.

Where do you run when life goes sideways and there is an emergency? What's your muster point? To my surprise, once I was back in right relationship with the Lord and in pursuit of God, I realized that I was still running to counterfeit muster points. None of these were a valid replacement for my faithful Lord!

You see, for longer than I would like to admit, I thought I was totally free. But that day as I saw that sign, I had a harsh reality check. Even though I intended for God to be my muster point, in actuality, He was *not the first place* I was running to.

Where do you run to? There is a story in the Bible about two women who were married to the same man. Their names were Rachel and Leah, and they were married to Jacob. You can find the story in Genesis chapter 29. Note especially what happens when children began to be born.

Even though there were different cultural norms of the day, it's hard to imagine two women being married to the same man! And, we think we have issues! Anyway, although Rachel was the favorite, she was unable to have children. God saw that Leah was treated with much less respect and value. He enabled her to start having children while the other woman, Rachel, could not. Check out the names of Leah's children and what they meant. The first one was Reuben, which means "Because the Lord has looked upon my affliction; and now my husband will love me."

The second child she named Simeon which means "God heard." She said, "The Lord has heard that I am hated; He has given me this son also." Then the third child came and she called him Levi which means "connect." She said, "Now *this* time my husband will be attracted to me, because I have given him three sons."

Do you see what's happening here? She was actually placing her self-confidence in the birth of each son to win her husband's heart. It wasn't working!

Then she had another baby and she called him Judah which means "Praise God." She said, "*This time* I will praise the Lord." She finally understood where she needed to run to find fulfillment. Little did Leah know that the Lord was working out a much bigger plan through the waiting womb of Rachel. God still had something special for Leah, He was simply monitoring her self-worth and value, because she was still in her own lane of striving. She did, however, ultimately come to the realization that this was not her battle, nor even a contest for her husband's favour.

After years of running to people and things to seek validation and approval, I finally realized that the only place I can truly find fulfillment in is the Lord. When I saw the sign that day, it hit me, "God, You are my muster point, my safe place. I now find my value, my self-worth and everything I need from You. That is the only way I can continue on when my life gets turned upside down or when others let me down."

What about during the COVID-19 pandemic? That situation left us in a state of emergency like nothing we have ever known. Who and what did you run to for safety and protection? And did it provide you the comfort you needed? Maybe the people or places you ran to for comfort or safety were no longer accessible? Or, maybe they were no longer comforting to you. Maybe you experienced something worse, like losing a job or a family member?

During the pandemic someone asked me, "How do you sustain your strength to keep pouring out?" And in short, I just said, "I keep running to the Source; I know where to run to for what I need." I like what my pastor said one time: "God wants us to live *from* rest not *for* rest."

Regretfully, there are many who know Jesus, yet don't know Jesus as their muster point. And the only way I have been able to keep going or to keep pouring out is by running to my Heavenly Father. He alone is my muster point and my safe place.

I remember I was in the middle of an unexpected but very heartbreaking situation and I couldn't find any peace or comfort to resolve it. Vaughan thought about my struggle and said: "I read somewhere about a family who spent one hour reading their Bible or praying for every hour of T.V. they watched. It was to help keep their life balanced." Wow! I knew he wasn't trying to judge me, but it did help to adjust my perspective to view God as my muster point.

Another time, I remember receiving a message from my editor where she wrote, "I felt that I needed to tell you to 'step off the hamster wheel and keep moving forward.'" There was never a more powerful word spoken at the perfect time. "Step off the hamster wheel." I was not only running to the wrong places, I was allowing my mind to keep running in circles, and it was keeping me stuck.

Where do you run to? I believe God is asking us a weighty question today. What is your muster point? Are you tired of running to people and things that leave you feeling empty, frustrated, or worse? Tired of living without joy or contentment because God isn't the place you run to? Tired of not being able to move forward because you can't let go of your past hurts or anxious thoughts?

You see, until I was stripped of the things I ran to for my validation or approval, I would never have been able to grow in confidence and trust in the only validation or approval that matters—His! Don't get me wrong, we do need people. We need support but, they can't be the *source* of our strength.

Someone asked me in an interview once, "Do you have a spiritual mentor that you go to for guidance?" And, "What do you find special or important about these kinds of relationships?"

I responded, "God gives us people for reasons and seasons, but God is *my Person*."

Honestly, I like to look at all my relationships like the *proper* use of a credit card. When the money is there in my account, then I can make choices about how I want to use it. All is well. However, if I exceed my limit or exhaust my funds on things that should have been reserved for other commitments, I am pulling from an empty well while falling deeper into it.

Do you see how that relates to drawing from other people? If I'm continuing to withdraw strength or encouragement from others which I can only receive from the Lord, I'll always feel empty and frustrated. My dependency is misplaced. As a result, I put way too much pressure on my relationships as I endeavor to receive what I should have been withdrawing from the Lord.

Jesus says in Matthew 5:6 *"Blessed are those who hunger and thirst for righteousness, for they shall be satisfied." (ESV)* When you hunger for God, you will run to Him and you will never be left empty. And when you're strong in Him, you are then ready to have those healthy, strong relationships that you are so desperate for.

Yes, there are people who will graciously hang on to you, or "breathe for you" in times when you can't, like Vaughan did for me. But that can only last so long. Eventually you will need to learn to access the strength that only God can provide for yourself. Are you ready to make Jesus your muster point today? You'll find there's no safer place to run.

Chapter 14

Keeping in Step

Do you remember that children's game: Red Light-Green Light 1-2-3? You can play with as few as 2, but obviously the more the better. One person is chosen to stand at the front with his or her back to the group and to act as the traffic light. That person then says, (as slow or as fast as they feel to) "Red light-green light 1-2-3" and then turns around. The players have to run as fast as they can until the person giving the command turns around on 3. The object of the game is to see who will be the first to get to the front without getting caught moving. If you are caught moving, you will have to start over.

If you're lucky enough to stop and not get caught, the next challenge is waiting until you hear the command again before moving. The person who does the best at this game is the person who is really good at *listening, waiting, and obeying the instructions*—all the while heeding the *"timing."* Some people even get sent back during the waiting because they were caught moving before the one giving the command had his or her back turned again. If you are caught moving, you can complain and get frustrated, but the fact is you must start over if you don't follow the guidelines of the game.

I have come to understand that same principle is true in my journey with the Lord. Sometimes He says, "Go." Sometimes He will say, "Stop." And at other times He will say, "Wait." However, learning to trust Him through that process is the hard part, especially when you *know* you heard, "Green light!" Why is He now telling me to stop? We learn quickly that this is not a game but actually very central to our walk with the Lord. Parallels from this game have helped me learn to *keep in step* with the Lord.

As I have shared with you from my story, I spent six years running from the Lord. But, after I surrendered to Him, God not only took my brokenness but also showed me a better life. He replaced the brokenness with so much passion. I knew without a shadow of a doubt that I was meant to share my story with the world. But, even with that passion and vision, I didn't have an audience to share it with. I'm just a small-town girl from Newfoundland Labrador. Who would want to listen to me? Besides a few family and friends, who could I tell?

There were many places or platforms that I was convinced that I *should* be on, but time and time again the door would remain closed. How could I be so right about hearing "green light" from God, and yet be seeing an even brighter *red light*? I would see other people leading and using their gifts and wonder why *I* had to wait. Many times in my prayers (or my one-way conversations to God) I would say; "How can You give me this passion without a platform?"

I didn't understand the red light. That red light was causing me a lot of frustration, and I kept telling Him," I'm ready when you are, God! But please help me wait."

It was the summer of 2011 when God opened a door for my friend and me to go to Newfoundland Labrador to do some speaking. We were heading to my parents' church where they pastored. We both grew up in the same town, and our first stop was the church of our childhood. So, let's just say, it was a *safe* place to *practice*.

We had an amazing time on that tour home. However, the irony of it all was when my friend and I were on the flight home. I turned to her and said, "I am emotionally, physically and spiritually exhausted. If *this* is the amount of energy that's required for this type of ministry, then I don't think I can do it." I was getting the "platform" I was *so* desperate to receive, yet here I was saying, "I don't want it!" Do you know what God spoke into my heart in that moment? "GOOD!" I was like, "*What*? What do you mean, "*good*"?" He said, "Now you are beginning to understand the waiting and how waiting is even more important than the going." He followed it up with "*You* can't, but with *my* strength, *you can*!"

I grew up going to church a minimum of 3 times a week and I had graduated from Bible College. But until *that* moment, I didn't truly understand what it meant to "*wait*" upon the Lord. I had never understood what it meant to allow Him to renew my strength. Waiting had always been this painful thing that *always* felt like a "*no*" in my mind. I would read my Bible and pray, but I never understood what it meant to come to God for my daily food for spiritual strength. I didn't know what it was to "walk in step with Him" allowing Him to lead or give the instructions. I am embarrassed to admit I was that person who wanted the "results" of the fit body without putting in time in the gym. I wanted the platform but didn't have the character or deep roots to stand on that platform. Nor did I truly understand what was required of me to be strong enough to stand there.

It was through that experience that God showed me that my platform was everywhere I set my foot. And, in order for Him to work *through* me, He first had to work *in* me. Trust me, you never want your platform to outgrow your character or faith in God. It was shortly after that trip that I really started making time daily with the Lord. I couldn't believe the difference it was making in me. While it wasn't an overnight change, I did start to feel my heart change.

This new shift in my heart caused me to start looking for ways to serve God in my everyday life. God was teaching me what it was to first lead myself before I could ever lead others. That meant I was to simply keep in step with Him as I walked out my Christian life. One thing that I'll say now that you'll probably hear me say again and again is this: "God is much more concerned with what He is doing *in* you than what He does *through* you."

So, before He gives you a green light to follow the passion in your heart, you can be certain He'll make *sure* you're ready to receive it. At times you may feel like He's taking it back or saying no. You might even begin to question if you heard Him correctly from the beginning. This is especially true if you don't understand how to prepare to receive your God-given passions and dreams. And if you push forward without waiting for Him, that will be something that most certainly will "send you back" to the start, just like in the childhood game.

Long before I even knew the words of Galatians 5:25 that tell us "*if we live by the Spirit, let us also walk by the Spirit*" *(NASB)*, God was teaching me to *keep in step* with Him.

Learning to Listen

This season of learning to keep in step with the Lord was also when He was teaching me to listen. Listening is the first step in being able to follow instructions. And, as I have mentioned before, this is an area that I have really struggled with. "God is that you?" And, when you start tuning your ears to listen to the Lord, there will be other voices that will try to distract or derail you.

I remember a time when I was bombarded with negative thoughts and I didn't know how to discern the truth with regard to the decisions I was trying to make. I was so overwhelmed and couldn't quiet the noise in my head. It was in that time that I had a dream. I was in a room and there was just chaos and noise. The room was filled with people yelling at me, telling me what "they thought" I should be doing. I was getting more and more overwhelmed and confused. It was so loud; I couldn't think straight. As the noise got louder and louder, in the distance I began to hear ever so lightly a voice saying, "*Listen, listen.*" And the more I focused on the still, small voice, the quieter the chaos and noise around me became. Little by little I began to clearly hear the word "listen." Finally, the only thing I could hear was, "*LISTEN.*" And the chaos was gone.

I woke up from that dream with the words "My sheep hear my voice" repeating in my mind. I found the scripture in John 10:27-28, *"My sheep hear my voice, and I know them, and they follow me: And I give unto them eternal life; and they shall never perish, neither shall any man pluck them out of my hand." (KJV)* God was trying to get me to listen to Him over the confusion and chaos that often overwhelmed me. But honestly, I wasn't yet grounded in God's Word. I didn't understand the value of being in God's Word and developing the discipline that would actually help me to hear. Only then could I be confident in what I was hearing so I could keep in step with Him. If we stay focused on the Shepherd's voice, we will never go astray.

Obedience

My journey may be different than yours, but the principles of what's required remain the same: Red light green light, (1) obedience, (2) faith, and (3) discipline. Never again do I want to get distracted by my own pain with the result that I can't hear or discern the Father's voice from all the others. When you start to be obedient in the small things God ask you to do, you will be obedient to do the bigger things He ask.

When my friend and I were in Newfoundland Labrador on that speaking trip, I remember we were driving around one of the small towns. As we were driving, I looked and saw a man sitting on his front porch. When I saw him, I instantly felt we needed to stop and say hi. I didn't know what we would say; I just had this feeling that he was lonely. We circled back around, got out of the car, and went over to him. We told him who we were and why we were in town. I casually mentioned that I felt to stop and say hi. The first words out of his mouth were, "Thank you so much. I sit here day after day and no one says hi to me. I feel so lonely." We stayed and talked a little while. I told him that my dad was a pastor and gave him his number and said he could call anytime. I assured him that my dad would love to come and have coffee with him. He was so blessed that day, and you can be sure that we were also. Obedience in these little things help us trust God and obey in the bigger things. Like being okay to wait, stop, or be brave enough to go. It's about *keeping in step*.

Faith

When I was in the beginning stages of writing my first book. I had no deadline set nor timetable. To be honest, from the day I said, "I have decided to write a book" to the time I actually sat down to begin writing was 3 months." Yup! I was so scared. My husband knew this, which was why he challenged me to set a deadline. So, I did. I connected with the editor I was working with at that time and told her my idea of a summer/fall launch in

2015. I asked her if this was possible. I took a step of faith not knowing what would happen.

Within a half hour of sending my message to her, I received this response, "Vahen, I am so sorry to have to tell you this, but I am struggling with the biggest bout of depression I have dealt with for years. I am unable to help you reach that deadline. I am so sorry that I am letting you down. I would completely understand if you choose to get someone else to help you."

Without hesitation, I knew I was not to move on toward my deadline. Rather, I needed to support her where she was. My book could wait. My response to her was: "I am so sorry that you are struggling this way. I want you to know that I will not be getting anyone else." I continued, "I feel God wants me to love and support you and not move on." I said, "I know that if I were to move on, I don't deserve to write this book."

What an amazing experience for us both. She felt supported and loved when she needed it the most. And, I was growing in understanding how to keep in step and walk by faith. Yes, I knew that I got a green light to write my book, but now I had to have faith to wait and trust God for His perfect timing. And He totally had the best timing. God brought another editor along when it was time to transition. The transition had nothing to do with me meeting a deadline. It was a decision she had to make. And, it was about both of us realizing that she would not be able to continue. As I said before, God is much more concerned with what He is doing *in* us than what He is doing *through* us.

Sometimes waiting in faith is just that: trusting God, no matter what. It's in the waiting that we have the biggest temptation to take things into our own hands. But when we are in step with Him, we can be sure we'll stay on the right path and avoid unnecessary frustration. My understanding of Proverbs 3:5 is this; When you trust in the Lord with all your heart and not on your own understanding and you acknowledge Him in all your ways, He *will* direct your path.

Discipline

Here's that "D" word again. Let's go back to that moment on the flight home and my statement to the Lord, "If *this* is the amount of energy that's required for this type of ministry, then I don't think I can do it." That was the turning point of when I began to understand the necessity of discipline in a new way. Discipline is the glue that will *keep* you *keeping in step*. God plainly said, "Y*ou* can't, but with *my* strength, *you can*!" He was introducing me to how important it was to be with Him daily.

During that season that my father-in-law mentioned in conversation about the different ways he read the Bible through to get a different perspective. He said, "Sometimes I read it chronologically and other times topically, etc." I was convicted because I was embarrassed to admit I hadn't ever read it all the way through from front to back. I had graduated from Bible College, but not once did I feel the need to read the Word all the way through. My Bible reading consisted of whatever scripture was in the devotional I was reading that day. At other times I would "attempt" a Bible-in-a-year plan, but never was successful. I would read the parts I liked, or when I felt like it. What was wrong with that? At least I was reading *something*. And while that was a great way to start, it was not enough if I wanted to grow deeper. So, that's when I determined that this was the year that I *would* read the Bible through cover to cover.

I will be completely honest with you and say that starting was not that bad. I've done that before. But, the test came when I endeavored to be consistant with reading even when I didn't "feel" like it. That's when it got tough. There were times when I felt I was just reading words on a page. I wasn't hearing anything; maybe a few crickets. But as I pressed through and stuck to my goal, I was developing discipline. It was just like hitting that wall when you start working out. If you don't push past it, you will quit. But this time I was *not* quitting. Eventually I started seeing and hearing God in little ways. I would start to see scripture speak to me on the day that I needed it. Coincidence? I don't think so.

However, my biggest discovery was as I neared the end of my one-year reading plan. My first thought was, "Yay, I did it!, now I can go back to what I did before." But, even as I thought that, something inside me screamed, "No!" I realized that the Word of God wasn't just a "task to complete," but it had become my daily bread. I was being sustained and nurtured by God and His words. This time spent with Him became the food that helped me grow strong. I was developing the discipline not to quit and my roots were growing deeper. I understood as John 15:5 states that *"apart from Him I can do nothing." (NIV)* He was right, I couldn't do this ministry in my own strength. The thing is, I didn't realize that's what I had been attempting! I was like those seeds on the rocky path. I didn't have deep roots and so when times got tough, I would get swept away.

You might have all the same questions that I have had. "How long do I have to wait before I can_____? Or, "How long do I have to suffer in this pain?" My journey may be different than yours, but the principles of what's required remain the same; Red light-green light, (1) obedience, (2) faith, and (3) discipline. Let me repeat my declaration: *"Never again do I want to get distracted by my own pain that stops me from discerning the Father's voice or that keeps me out of step with Him."*

1. Write down something you are waiting on an answer for.

_____

_____

_____

_____

_____

_____

_____

2. Do you find it hard to "quiet the noise?" If so, when was the last time you sat in silence with the Lord and asked Him what He thought?

_____

_____

_____

_____

3. My challenge is for you to ask God some questions and sit with Him to test out your hearing. And then, when He speaks, be obedient and step out in faith. Oh, and don't forget to journal your experience.

_____

_____

_____

_____

If you would like a guide for your prayer time, here is a listening prayer exercise that I think will help you as you are learning to listen and keep in step.

Prayer Exercise

How many of you have experienced God speaking to you other than by a scripture? Like a dream? An inspirational message? Or just a still small voice like I described above? Other?

_____

_____

_____

_____

Is there something that you have been wanting to ask God? Write down your question, and then under it just start writing what comes to mind.

_____
_____
_____
_____
_____

If you don't have a question, maybe consider asking one of the following questions:

Is there someone you want me to give a word of encouragement to?

_____
_____
_____
_____
_____

What would you want to say to them?

_____
_____
_____
_____
_____
_____
_____

What would you like me to stop doing, start doing, or do differently in my life? What steps should I take for doing this?

_____

_____

_____

_____

_____

I would like to suggest you to consider spending a set amount of time everyday to sit and talk with God. You can ask your own questions or use the ones I've suggested above. You also might want to go back and review the additional exercise that I included about goal setting with the balance wheel to help you in your time with the Lord. Don't feel bad if you don't hear anything right away. It takes time to quiet the noise. Remember, He's more eager to speak than we are to listen! As you practice listening, you'll find it easier to keep in step.

Section 5

A Courageous Perspective

<u>Face The Waves</u>

They say this journey won't be easy
They say I will sink if I try
They say I better row to shore now
But You say you're by my side
I won't turn around I won't run
I'll ride into the flood

Courage don't mean I'm not afraid
Courage don't mean I'm not shaking on my way
Though waters rise and raging tides
Keep pounding me all day
Courage means I'll face the waves I'll face the waves

I know I heard Your voice calling
I know I can reach for Your hand
I know this journey won't be easy
But I know You're by side
I won't run away I won't hide
I'll sail into the tide

Though water's rising
Though storms are raging
Though fear is calling I'll face the waves
Though water's rising
Though storms are raging
I know tides are turning I'll face the waves[1]

1   Face The Waves, Chelsea Amber, CD Baby (on behalf of Chelsea Amber); CD Baby Sync Publishing (2018)

There's Always Another Way

Have you ever said, "My mind is made up and that's it!" "I'm not budging." Then someone comes along and provides you with new information and with a convincing case for why you should consider another point of view. And you think, "I didn't see it that way before." Or what about your mood? Has someone ever changed your mood, either for the good or the bad?

My husband has this uncanny ability to make me laugh when I don't want to. When Vaughan and I first started traveling after the virus paralyzed my lower body, my first trip to the airport in my wheelchair was quite the experience. We went to the baggage counter and the lady told me that I would have to check my "cool" chair with the baggage and sit in an ugly oversized grey wheelchair with a bright orange flag waving at about 6 feet above me. I was about to *lose* it. Vaughan saw the tears in my eyes and knew I was about to have "a moment." So he leaned over and said, "It's okay sweetie, they save all the ugly chairs for the pretty girls." I went from almost bawling my eyes out to laughing.

Yes, it *was* great that he shifted my perspective in that moment amidst the flow of what is now my "normal life." In the early stages I couldn't see past my disability and how it was now defining me. I was consumed with fear and insecurity daily. The perspective I had about myself (and everything in my life) was that it was this big, hopeless mess.

I think of all the things that cause us to keep the perspective of fear, worry, or overwhelming anxiety. The list is endless, but *my* discovery is that our perspective of ourselves, our circumstances, and yes, even our perspective of God can limit us and hold us back from receiving full freedom. I'm praying that I can provide you with some new information that will help you change your perspective of each of these areas if you're willing to see there is another way!

Change your view of self

When I was first paralyzed, I spent the majority of my time and energy focusing on all the things I *couldn't* do. I was limited because I didn't want to do things if I couldn't do *it like I did before.* That approach was keeping me stuck. It left me feeling even more insecure and overwhelmed. This mindset affected everything and limited my independence *even more*.

I remember saying, "I don't want to drive again until I can use my feet." I wanted desperately to be independent, yet I refused to do it differently than I did it before. I had the perspective that doing it differently made me less of a person. This perspective was more paralyzing than my disability or the chair I was in. When I started seeing other people who had less mobility than me doing far more than I was doing, I realized my view of myself was holding me back. I knew I had a choice to make. Do I stay focused on what I *can't* do and remain stuck, or shift my focus to what I *can* do?

I wanted to drive, but to move past my self-imposed limitations, I had to find another way. If I refused the "other way" I would not be driving. That choice to accept driving with hand controls instead of my feet gave me so much independence. This independence unlocked some freedom in me and boosted my confidence. This change in perspective enabled me to have courage to try other things. Now, not only am I driving, but I have been rock climbing, downhill skiing, zip-lining, and skydiving. And that list of physical achievements does not even mention becoming an author, motivational speaker, and starting my own non-profit organization. I may not be able to do things the way I used to, but I know now there *is* more than one way if you're willing to see and accept it.

I returned home from running errands one day, pulled into my garage, got out of my car and rolled onto the lift that allows me to access my house without having to climb stairs. Well, the keypad to the side door of my house didn't work. Apparently the battery in the keypad died and it wouldn't let me enter the code to get in. Yes, I could have called my neighbor to come. I could have called any number of my amazing friends who are always so willing to help me. There were times in the past that I have, but this particular time I had this thought: "I bet I can get in that front door!"

So, I went around to the front door, got out of my chair, and "bummed" my way up the steps. Stretching as far as I could, I managed to unlock the front door. I then proceeded to "worm" my way into my house and unlock the garage door. Then sliding back down the steps, I got up into my chair and returned to the garage to access the open door. Yay, mission accomplished! I couldn't get into my house the way I had before, but I found that there is always another way. Like the old saying goes: "Where there is a will there is a way!"

These stories might not seem like life-changing situations to you, but for me they were! There was a time when I actually needed two nurses to change me. That process always left me feeling like I would never get my confidence (or dignity) back. This was compounded by being told that I would always have to be dependent on others for my personal care and mobility. Now, every step forward is a valued treasure to me. Gaining my independence in these areas again, after seemingly losing it through the initial paralysis *was* life changing.

My husband told me about an experience his dad had when he visited India many years ago. He described how the locals were moving dirt in bags on their shoulders from one location to another nearby. John asked them why they did it that way rather than using a wheelbarrow. He soon realized they didn't even know what a wheelbarrow was. Without that equipment, their way was the way they always did it.

I guess this illustration could be used with us in life. People naturally don't like change, but God knows there is another way—a *better* way. That "better" (but yet unknown) way holds the potential to bring improvement to our lives. Once we discover the "better way" we must then be willing to accept it. If I didn't change my perspective and find another way to view myself or my circumstances, I would still be at home on my couch consumed with fear and depression. I never would have discovered that I have access to this extra strength and courage.

I believe that car trouble or things breaking down in general is something that follows me more than the average "Joe." However, whether you are willing to find another way to view the situation or not, we can agree they make for some great stories after the fact.

One morning I was up and ready for a full day of meetings. My first meeting was across town. Since I pride myself in being on time, I was actually ready and heading out earlier than usual. I went to start my car but, unfortunately the battery was dead. I quickly called roadside assistance and thought that maybe I could still get to my meeting on time. That truly was wishful thinking on my part! Before long I was beginning to get frustrated by this disruption, but I thought to myself, "I can't change it, so I might as well embrace it." I even prayed that God would help me be okay with the delay and help me overcome the frustration of now missing my first meeting.

The gentleman who came to help with my car had to get something out of my trunk and saw my box of books. With excitement he asked: "Hey, that's you on the cover. Did you write this book?" Well, that sparked a wonderful conversation that included him sharing his own "pain journey." He ended by saying how honored he was to have met me. He thanked me for the courage to keep going so that others can also be encouraged to keep going.

Looking for different ways to view myself or my situation has indeed given me a courageous perspective. I also found out afterward, that missing that meeting turned out to be a blessing in disguise. Without getting into all the details, I'll just say I'm glad there was a "better way" for my morning to begin, even though at first I had been frustrated. Without the Lord's "better way" I would have missed out on a beautiful experience and the opportunity to see my situation "another way."

Do you feel trapped in the emotions you are feeling because of the way you view yourself, or your situation? I think about of all the things that you may have experienced in your life and especially in the COVID-19 season. These things may be causing you anxiety as you stay focused on all the things you can't control. I want to challenge you to look at that obstacle or giant in your path and tell yourself, "There *is* always another way."

Please allow yourself time to sit and reflect on your current mindset or situation as you consider these questions.

1. What negative view do you have about yourself or your circumstance that is obstructing your ability to find another way?

_____

_____

_____

_____

_____

2. What one thing can you do today that can help you consider the possibility of another way?

_____

_____

_____

_____

_____

3. What positive effect do you think that your courage to find another way could have on someone else?

_____

_____

_____

_____

_____

"For God has not given us a spirit of fear, but of power and of love and of a sound mind." 2 Timothy 1:7 (NKJV)

Chapter 16

You Can Make Extraordinary Ordinary!

What do you consider extraordinary? Is it something like jumping out of an airplane or speaking in front of thousands of people? What extraordinary thing do you think you could *never* do? Perhaps the two things I've mentioned aren't on the top of your extraordinary list. Maybe it's the idea of having courage to face that person at work or a bully at school. What is that "thing" you think you can't do? What if I told you that you can make extraordinary become just ordinary for you in your everyday. Would you want that kind of courage? Yes, even your tragic circumstances come with an opportunity to experience the extraordinary! I am suggesting a slight (!) change in your thinking to help give you a courageous perspective. You can see it is possible.

When I got my diagnosis from the doctor and was told I'd never walk again, walking not only *seemed* impossible, I was told it *was* impossible. I wasn't even able to dress myself yet; so, for me, standing was definitely extraordinary! When I heard that report, something inside me screamed, "*No!*" I simply did not want to accept this. I began to tell everyone that I *would* walk the aisle on my wedding day. I even had a nurse approach my mom and say she felt I wasn't thinking clearly and then suggested I seek professional help.

True, my circumstance was very bleak, but I was determined to walk the aisle on my wedding day. I had no idea if I ever *could*, but I was not going to give up hope. And I had to try. I made the choice not to focus on the doctor's report and was determined to create a new reality for myself. And I did it! Can you imagine how incredible it was for me when I *stood* for the first time? If there was Instagram back then, that video would have gone viral! Standing that first time made me think: "If I did *that*, what else could I do?"

So, I set some goals and was determined to do more. Then, one year after the doctors said I would never walk again, I walked down the aisle to meet my groom on our wedding day. When I *walked* down that aisle in a gripping and emotional ceremony with my mom and dad on either side of me, *standing* became so *what*? You guessed it: *ordinary!*

I've spent far too long letting the fear of my circumstances hold me prisoner. I had to change the way I viewed myself *and* circumstances or I would never be able to move forward.

Are you facing something that seems impossible? Maybe you don't feel you are capable of making extraordinary ordinary. I would like to pause here and ask you to reflect again for just a moment on the question I asked in chapter 6. *"What's Stopping You?"* If you could do anything, if money was no object and you had no barriers in your way, what would your response be? What is your extraordinary?

I promise you that if you tell yourself you can't, you won't. But if you tell yourself you *can*, you *will* make the extraordinary be an everyday, ordinary occurrence.

Let's share some journaling moments together. Write down at least one thing that you want to do but you feel you can't. Write it as if you are already doing it. I have provided an example below of my extraordinary. Would you be willing to share your extraordinary? Then, write out a few small tasks that you could do to accomplish your dream. You don't have to do them all in one day, but these small things you've listed will position you to make one step towards your courageous goal. Remember, start small. Notice in my example below that I will also share a current huge challenge! Just because!

My Extraordinary:
My story is inspiring others and empowering them to choose courage.

Todays task:
1. Begin everyday by telling myself that I do have a story to tell.
2. Look for opportunities in which I can share with people, even if it's at the mall or a coffee shop.

3. Stop telling myself I can't, or that I am not enough.

My Extraordinary:
I am not afraid of bee's (Deathly afraid!)

Today's task:
1. I will go outside and sit on my patio at least once this week for 5 minutes, and not run inside at the sight of a bee.
2. Summertime when driving, I will roll my window down at least once, and not roll it up when stopping at a red light or stop sign.

If any thoughts come, either from your own mind or the words of others that contradict your task, I want you to tell yourself: "It's a lie!" And repeat your statement often. I literally have to say, "I am not afraid of bees!" Do this every day or every time you are battling in that area. One day you will believe it, because we will always believe the "thing" we keep repeating to ourselves. Remember: if you keep saying, "I can't, you won't."

Now it's your turn!

My Extraordinary:

_____
_____
_____
_____

Today's task:

_____
_____
_____
_____

Fear of Bees and Courageous Me

While I have completed this now in some areas, I have just started to apply it to help me get over my fear of bees. Why? First, because I never even considered that I *could* get over my fear of bees. And secondly, I've not had the slightest desire to try. I thought it was impossible. Funny how I refused the doctor's diagnosis when he said I would never be independent or walk again, but I continue to accept my fear of bees!

One summer when Vaughan and I were living in Ontario, we went out to get lunch. He went into the store and I stayed in the car. Keep in mind: it's almost a "law" in our world that we never leave windows down when Vahen is left in the car alone. She can't just run away, right? Well, the next thing I know there is this small, yet very ugly yellow thing buzzing towards me. "Someone" forgot to close his window all the way! I thought I was going to lose my mind. I didn't think twice before I opened the door to the car and climbed out like spider-man from our car and latched onto the car beside us.

I didn't have enough strength to get very far. But when I was close enough to grab that other vehicle, I hung on for dear life—wondering when my legs would give out. My arms were really getting a workout. And all I was thinking was, "Please let Vaughan come back before the owner of this car!"

That would have been ideal. However, a young man approached the car that I was draped over with a puzzled look on his face. I thought, "busted!" I really didn't know where to begin to explain why I was not only near his car but draped over it. So, in full speed I said, "I'm in a wheelchair and I am deathly afraid of bees. My husband left the window down in our car, so I am fleeing for my life!" As I was explaining to him that I was not trying to vandalize his car, nor was I a crazy stalker lady, Vaughan returned. He helped me get back to safety, but not before having a little chuckle with the gentleman at my expense.

You would think I am allergic to bees or maybe have been stung by them, but nope! I am just terrified of the little critters. The summer of July 2020, I was telling my friend about another time when my fear of bees nearly caused an accident. I was driving. My husband's window was down on the passenger side. Then it happened! A bee flew right in through his open window. It's funny because we were actually just talking about my book, *Contagious Courage,* when the bee came in. It flew right under the steering wheel. I did tell you I was driving, right? I started hyperventilating and nearly passed out. I couldn't jump out this time. My *"Prince Charming,"* said, "Sweetie, you are an overcomer. You have courage to overcome your fear of bees." Trying not to go off the road and trying my best to remain "calm," I said, "Okay." And, I actually yelled, *"THIS IS NOT THE TIME TO TELL ME NOT TO FEAR BEES!"*

As I related the story to my friend that day, she really challenged me to change my approach to my fear. As I talk to you about your very real situations that are holding you back, I have now begun to believe that *I can* and *I am willing to try!* Are you with me?

While I am not *completely* over my fear of bees, I have been practicing my "assignment" and repeating "I'm not afraid of bees." And it's been helping. Did this work the first 5 times? No! But I am proud to say that I don't run or freak out as quickly. This is more than convincing myself. With each time I say it, I am making a choice. I am reinforcing what is possible. I'm reducing my expectation of a fearful outcome and I'm believing for a better response. I'm also agreeing with the Lord's promise to me that He is with me and will never leave me. Yes, it is making a difference. And I am confident it will work for you.

SIDE NOTE: *My* extraordinary is not *your* extraordinary! So please don't compare yourself to others. Let me help you put this into perspective by reminding you about what I mentioned before regarding goal-setting and not comparing your goals to others. Remember what I said. How silly would it be for me to compare my 11 unassisted steps to your 10,000 steps? I would be defeated before I begin.

But when I share my success of *any* steps without comparing myself to others, what happens is now *my* extraordinary has the power to encourage others to try.

The only way you and I can truly fight those negative thoughts and experience the extraordinary is by faith. We must believe that God can be trusted, otherwise I couldn't be obedient to do as He leads. My time with

God is super important to me. It's the only way I am able to continue to do the extraordinary in my "every day." Have you heard this scripture in Joshua 1:9? It tells us *"Be strong and courageous!" (NIV)* Psalm 139:14 tells us, *"That we are fearfully and wonderfully made," (NKJV)* and that we are loved. What's more powerful than having the God of all the universe tell you that you are loved and wonderfully created? I have grown to trust those words and it has indeed helped me be strong and courageous.

If you truly believe what God says about you, then you won't be so affected by what others think. Nor will you constantly doubt yourself because of all the negative self-talk. Trust me when I tell you, you *can* make extraordinary things become ordinary in your everyday. Are you ready to try?

A Reboot Changes Everything

Have you ever had your computer freeze up on you? Frustrating, isn't it? You're going along and next thing you know your programs are all frozen and you can't do anything. You can sit there and stare at it or even yell at it, but the fact is that unless you do a reboot, your computer is useless. I wonder how many of you need a reboot in *your* life? Maybe circumstances outside of your control have caused you to shut down or lose faith? You're stuck in a perspective that God is not a loving God. Or maybe you're stuck in believing that nothing good will ever happen for you. If rebooting allows the computer to restart and get back to working normally, *what if having a reboot of your perspective of God could restore what you've lost?* What if you could get back to believing who He *truly* is or, maybe believe for the first time. What if the truth about God began to empower you to receive more than you ever dreamed possible? What if you had a courageous perspective?

When I went to Bible College I had high hopes with big dreams. I even made this bold statement. "God, I'll go through *anything* as long as I know you're with me." I had this expectation of what I thought my dream would look like. When transverse myelitis took my independence and nearly destroyed me, it also took my ability to dream. What remained was a perspective that nothing good could ever come from my life now.

I'm guessing I'm not the only one who has cried out to God and accused Him of not caring because He didn't take your pain. Or perhaps you misinterpreted His seeming lack of response to remove you from a circumstance you were so desperate to escape. Maybe you concluded that to mean He didn't care.

How many times in my life have I quoted 2 Corinthians 12:9. *"My grace is sufficient for you, for my strength is made perfect in weakness. Therefore, I will boast all the more gladly about my weakness so that Christ's power may rest on me." (NIV)* Yes, I could quote it, but I can tell you I did not understand it. My perspective was limiting me and my ability to see God's power. That limitation was keeping me stuck. I needed a reboot of my thinking. I couldn't see past my circumstances. I firmly adopted this perspective of God and it was blocking my understanding of His power. As a result, I could not see what He could possibly do with all my weakness and all my pain.

I finally got desperate and said, *"OK, God, You take my pain; take my need for control. Take my pride and take my fear that I can never amount to anything. If you can do anything with this mess, go ahead."* And guess what? He did. He gave me a reboot. He changed my perspective. I started to view myself, my circumstances, and God differently. As a result, He was able to do more in me than I ever thought I was capable of. Because of the reboot I received I was able to see my wheelchair as a platform of hope.

I think about that story in 2 Kings 6:8-23 about Elisha that really relates to how we can get consumed by our view of ourselves or circumstances. More importantly, it reveals what happens when God steps in and does a reboot of our thinking that helps us have a courageous perspective. Elisha was giving the Israelite leadership a heads-up about when and where the Arameans would attack. Then his nation of Israel always held the advantage. The king of Aram was enraged and even accused his own men of being traitors. But they told him, "No, it's not us; it's Elisha. God is the One who tells Elisha what you say in your bedroom." So, the king went out to kill Elisha in the city where he and his young servant were staying.

When the Arameans arrived to kill Elisha, they totally surrounded the city with troops, horses, and chariots ready to attack. It was Elisha's young servant who brought the alarming word to the prophet. He told him that they were surrounded by the enemy. His urgent question was, "What shall we do?" Elisha's answer made very little sense to the young man, "Do not fear. Those who are with us are more than those who are with them."

Elisha then prayed, "Open his eyes, Lord, so that he may see." The Lord opened the servant's eyes and he looked and saw the hills full of horses and chariots of fire surrounding the army of the Arameans. The passage concludes with the unique victory the Lord brought to those trusting in Him.

If you don't reboot your view of God, you will never truly move past the insecurities and the circumstances that continue to surround and consume you. You will remain stuck and never really experience the extraordinary things God wants you to experience. God wants you to have peace. He wants you to know that no matter what circumstances are surrounding you, that *He is surrounding you.* He is bigger than that giant you're facing. I think back to how afraid I was when my life fell apart and I couldn't see past my circumstances. But God opened my eyes to see things as He saw them and gave me a courageous perspective.

In order to receive this courageous perspective, I had to take every thought captive and believe God's truth over the lies. I had to stop telling myself that "I can't" or that "I am not enough." I had to change my perspective, or I would not have ever moved forward.

Unstoppable

I have a chart below with some scriptures that have helped me maintain my courageous perspective. I suggest that you read each one. Reading each one out loud is even better. Allow yourself to really hear the words you are speaking over yourself. Compare it to the lies you are hearing about yourself or speaking to yourself. Then go ahead and write it into the chart below. Even if you don't know scripture, you can use Google to help you. First write the lie, then write the opposite of that lie, and use Google to ask for scripture regarding your truth (bible.com). Before I was convinced and believed that I was loved, I would repeat these words—even without *feeling* it was making a difference. (Just like my, "I'm not afraid of bees" declaration). Yet I persisted in declaring the truth of the scriptures. I *knew* God loved me, but I didn't *feel* lovable. Much like when you don't feel hungry, but you know you need to eat. It's not always about what you *feel*, but rather it's about what you *know* you need. That's faith. These truths are now the spiritual food I need to consume daily. This nourishment not only keeps me going it enables me to be unstoppable

The Lie	The Truth
I am not worthy of love	1 John 3:3 - I AM WORTHY. I AM LOVED
I am not enough	Ephesians 1:6 - I am ACCEPTED
I can't I am not strong enough	2 Corinthians 10:5 - Take EVERY thought captive
I can't forgive myself	Colossians 1:4 - I AM FORGIVEN
Nothing can fill this void	Colossians 2:10 - I AM COMPLETE IN CHRIST
I will never have peace	Isaiah 26:3-4 says, "You will keep *him* in perfect peace, *whose* mind *is* stayed *on You,* Because he trusts in You

What's attacking your courage or chipping away at your hope? Don't let it keep you stuck. I know firsthand that if you don't believe the truth about yourself and "find another way," you'll remain stuck and never move forward. Because of the reboot I received, I was able to see my wheelchair as a platform of hope. I want to declare it again: *"You can't always control what happens to you but you can control how you respond."*

What I am experiencing now goes beyond anything I could have ever been bold enough to ask for. Never in my wildest dream would I have thought that something that nearly destroyed me would provide an opportunity for more than I could have ever hoped or dreamed. I pray today that you will allow God to give you a reboot that results in a courageous perspective. That changes everything!

Now it's your turn. What lies are you believing about yourself or your situation today? Is there something that you are facing that you can't see a way around?

The Lie	The Truth

Section 6

A Life of Contagious Courage

From You For You!

Its Your voice that called me from darkness
Its Your love that set me free
And every day You guide my way And never ever leave
Its Your mercies new every morning As You're overtaking me
So everyday Its You I thank For every good and perfect thing

But its not all just for me
You wrote a bigger story
And the circle is complete
As I use what you give to bring You glory

You are my source, I know Its your hand that feeds me
I am Your hand, to go to someone who needs me
All that I have
All that I am take and use me
Teach me to give
Teach me to live in that beauty
Cause everything I am And everything I've got
Its from You for You from You for You God

Its my ransom fully paid As I'm covered in your shade
And anything that I could bring
It all came from You anyway
And the simple test of love
Do we do the things You said
Cause faith that doesn't move is dead[1]

---

1   Dan Macaulay, *From You For You,* https://www.youtube.com/watch?v=BoiJZ8ZlsNE (2012)

What's Your New Normal?

Long before I had to adapt to my new normal *physically*, God was trying to give me the mindset of a new normal *spiritually*. The problem was that I didn't understand it. What does it even mean when someone says, "My new normal?" I've heard that phrase a lot recently. It is usually applied when something has happened in their life that turned their world upside down or knocked them sideways. In their attempt to make sense of it all, people often say, "I'm trying to find my new normal." Maybe some one has said it to you in your pain with the intention of trying to help; but the fact is, it doesn't.

I first experienced adapting to my "new normal" when I lost my independence. I have shared my story with you of how that new normal was suddenly thrust on me. You've also heard me relate how I was certainly *not* happy with it.

To this day, I think back to that elastic band illustration that my friend's dad spoke into my life when I first went away to Bible College. There I sat on the steps of the college in tears because I was in a situation that was far from normal for me. I was very uncomfortable. That illustration has proven to be more powerful than I could have ever imagined. Along my life journey I've discovered just how true those words really were. *Stretching is a necessary part of growth in order for God to take us farther.*

The key to the new normal God was introducing me to is the key I want you to receive today. *"Learn to be very comfortable with being uncomfortable."*

After I was paralyzed, I spent 9 months in a rehabilitation hospital. I remember the challenge of trying to dress on my own before I got up for the day from my bed. But then later in the day, the bigger frustration came when I wanted to nap. You see, I wasn't able to get back up onto the bed on my own. I hated having to keep asking for help just to have a nap. So, guess what? I learned how to sleep in very uncomfortable positions. The nurses would come in and find me still in my modified sitting position but sprawled out from the waist up with my face down on the bed and my arms above my head, sound asleep.

Do you remember that prayer that I prayed when I was in my first year in college? Long before I knew what it might mean I stood in front of the whole school and said "God, I'll go through anything as long as I know You're with me." No, I didn't know what was ahead, but I knew I would need His strength.

Our new normal doesn't need to be defined by fear. Our new normal does not have to end in being trampled under the foot of intimidation. Each circumstance presents an opportunity to get comfortable with being very uncomfortable! You don't need to be okay with being confined or threatened, but rather growing stronger under the pressure. And, we do gain that strength progressively. Yes, it's an intentional process.

Growing stronger under pressure matters. I have a friend who's an Olympian athlete. During the COVID-19 lock-down she commented that one of the greatest challenges she faced in regard to her training was finding ways to continue working on and improving her strength after all the gyms closed. It was both funny and incredible to see how adaptive she became to her new normal. This girl was pushing cars and ATVs, flipping tractor-sized tires and doing leg squats with pails of oil balanced on a metal bar across her shoulders. She utilized what was available to her, asked around for resources and help, and didn't let what she couldn't control stop her.

We may not all be training for the Olympics, but we can learn creative ways to gain strength under pressure. In order to grow stronger physically you add more resistance or you add more weight. If you were really good at lifting 5 pounds at the gym would you stay lifting 5 pounds? No, you know you would need to add the extra weight in order to build the muscle to grow stronger. You definitely have to train your body to be comfortable with being uncomfortable. But when it's internal or relating to our spiritual health and growth, we fight against it, don't we?

You mean God is causing our pain? No, just like God didn't make me sick (or cause COVID-19), He did allow it. He will use the pressures of your life and your unwelcome circumstances to help you grow. The key is whether we embrace His help or not.

There is a verse in Jeremiah 29:11 that we quote all the time, *"'For I know the plans I have for you,' says the LORD, 'They are plans for good and not for disaster, to give you a future and a hope.'" (NLT)* Although you might not feel hope coming from that verse now, or even believe it, there's much contained in that scripture. Go ahead and ask, "Why would God allow my circumstance if He said, "I don't want to harm you?" And if He wants to prosper us, why do we suffer?" I want to take you back a few verses.

The Israelites were sent into exile. The majority of the Israelites there had the freedom even under their captors to do as Jeremiah 29:5 says, *"Build homes, and plan to stay. Plant gardens and eat the food they produce. Marry and have children." (NIV)* But, the instructions also included in verse 6, *"Do not dwindle away!" (NLT)* He further instructed them, *"I want you to work for the peace and prosperity of the city."*

Even though the majority of the exiles were not harshly treated, yet they were still away from their homeland. If I'm not mistaken, God was telling them to be comfortable with being uncomfortable in exile! Oh, but by the way, don't dwindle away. Don't just sit and watch Netflix all day. There will be work to be done and a livelihood to be maintained. Plus, they were to work for the peace of the city. And, for us, too, we are to work for the peace of our family, and our world. This is the same principle Jesus shared in his story in Luke 19:13, *"Occupy till I come." (KJV)*

The Word of the Lord continues *"Pray to the Lord for it; for its welfare will determine your welfare."* He named the number of years of their exile and then declared, *"But then I will come and do for you all the good things I have promised."* Now you can see that the familiar and often quoted words fit into a much bigger context. *"'For I know the plans I have for you,' says the LORD, 'They are plans for good and not for disaster, to give you a future and a hope.'"* The Lord follows that verse with *"It's in those days when you pray, I will listen. If you look for me wholeheartedly, you will find me. I will be found by you," says the Lord. "I will end your captivity and restore your* fortunes. *I will gather you out of the nations where I sent you and will bring you home again to your own land." Jeremiah 29:14 (NLT)*

Yes, God is wanting us to be comfortable with being uncomfortable. But, His purposes are greater than just our own comfort (or lack thereof.) He works in us and through us so we can bring peace and hope to the world. So we can be stronger. So we know what it is to cry out to Him in prayer.

I don't know why we have to experience so much pain on this earth. But, have you considered that this is not our *ultimate* home; and, we will never be fully settled or comfortable until we are with Christ eternally? Through that lens our experiences in this life take on a very different conclusion. You might see me in a wheelchair and think that maybe I'm still in that prison, but I have never been more free.

Remember when I told you my body confined me to the bathroom for many hours a day for 16 years with no foreseeable way out? That was a form of prison for me. What did I gain from that time? More strength and courage than I ever knew existed. But what I didn't tell you was that my first book was literally written in that prison! While I hated my captivity, today I am ever so thankful. It produced in me something that could have never been produced without that intense pressure.

God wants us free and He wants us to stay free. Sometimes I think we misunderstand freedom as being called to "comfort." If you focus on your comfort level to monitor your freedom, it will limit your ability to adapt and be effective. If I didn't learn to be comfortable in my prison time, I would still be a prisoner emotionally even though I am physically free.

Comfortable With Being Uncomfortable

Since watching the very intense documentary featuring Mt Everest in 2015, I couldn't help but be drawn to the parallels of life and my relationship with the Lord. I could understand so much more about the necessity of adapting to a new normal!

Theses two quotes I found from "Lessons From Climbing Mount Everest

That Challenge Our Views of Success."[1] were just too good not to share. *"The mountains are the ultimate classroom"* said Levine. *"These expeditions force you to get to know yourself and to figure out how to perform when you are completely outside of your comfort zone. You learn that you can push yourself far beyond your self-perceived limits."* When I read that, I was like wow, that's been my whole life. God wasn't trying to destroy me; He was stretching me!

After another one of her climbs on Mt. Everest, Levine said, *"It's not about spending a couple of minutes up top, it's about the lessons you learned along the way and what you are going to do with that information to be better going forward. Because of my previous failure I knew a heck of a lot more about my pain threshold, and my risk tolerance. The only reason I made it up in 2010 when most people turned back, was because I had that failed experience in 2002."*

That is my stance now. Because of my failed experiences (and even my pain journey through the different choices of my life,) I have confidence that I will survive whatever mountain or giant I face. I know a whole lot more now about my pain tolerance, but more importantly I know a whole lot more about my new normal. And it's simply that I lean on God's strength and not my own.

It's time to ask those important questions again. Is God stretching you and stirring up your comfort zone today? What have you done under pressure? Are you letting anxiety, fear, or frustration about the things you can't control, control you? Are you aimlessly letting life pass you by, or are you letting the pressure grow you stronger? I want to encourage you to let God take you past the limits of what you previously envisioned, so He can take you farther than what you ever thought possible or dreamed. My challenge to you today is to get comfortable with being uncomfortable. Show the world that when you're put to the test, your faith grows stronger. May your new normal become "shining brighter even when or even if!"

---

1 Mandy Antoniacci, *Lessons From Climbing Mount Everest That Challenge Our Views of Success,* https://www.inc.com/mandy-antoniacci/critical-lessons-from-climbing-mount-everest-that-are-refining-leadership.html (Online 2021, January)

The Strength of My Weakness

How many of us have things we wish we could change about ourselves? I think it's pretty clear by now that we all have insecurities or weaknesses that we'd rather hide than share—let alone boast about! So, I wonder why we feel the need to always pretend.

Allow me to boast a little for a moment. I'm a terible spellar. I don't always say the right thing. And the best part of me is that I am in a wheelchair. Do you see what I did there? I just bragged about my weaknesses. (I also fought with my editor to let me keep the two misspelled words.)

We never boast about our weakness, do we? We live in a world where every Facebook post and Instagram story captures smiling faces and thrilling adventures. It's a picture-perfect world where we only highlight our "filtered" *strengths*!

Maybe you're thinking, "Vahen, I thought you wanted us to be strong and courageous?" That is exactly my point. You see, we may have missed the definition of *true strength and true courage.* Along my own journey in the process of understanding *me*, I would try to hide my insecurities and weakness. That mindset just left me frustrated and feeling worthless. I was in no way feeling strong or courageous. When you focus on all the things that you're *not* or try to portray someone you're *not*, it will always limit your potential and hold you back.

And, as you have already seen, I have battled with many of the same fears and insecurities that you may have. Maybe not *exactly* the same, but likely your list could include poor self-image or wondering if your life will matter. These were lies I believed about myself too. These lies formed the walls of my paralyzing prison. What were the steps out of that prison? While

I've just spent the last 5 sections giving you a glimpse of that painful process. The short version is that I had to choose to embrace my insecurities and push forward. This has enabled me to reach beyond my wildest dreams and live this life of contagious courage.

Was that process tough? Absolutely! Did you know that people with spinal cord injuries are more likely to suffer from depression and mental health issues because of the trauma of having your life do a total 180? And, if not treated, it can send you into a downward spiral and leave you feeling hopeless and worthless with results leading to depression and anxiety.[1]

Well that was my story. We all know transitions are tough. To believe that you feel valued or loved (after years of holding onto the lie that you are not) is a challenge that I understand can seem impossible. But let me assure you, it is not! It is possible for this transition to happen even if outside voices reinforce the "less-than" lie you have believed.

There is a story in the Bible about a man named Gideon. Many Israelites believed that their enemy's continuous victory over them for the last 6 years meant that this year would be no different as well. They had simply abandoned their fields and fled into the hills. Gideon didn't run, but he was hiding his harvest in a wine-press even as the enemy formed in the valley nearby.

I like several things about this story but let me tell you what I love the most. When God showed up while Gideon was in his weak and fearful state, God called him a *valiant warrior*! Are you kidding me? Gideon was, according to his own self-description, as far from living strong and courageous as you can imagine. Yet, God tells him he is a *valiant warrior.*

You see, God will always see you as you *will* be, not as you *are.* But I'm getting ahead of myself. Let's read on in the story, picking up right where God meets Gideon. Seated under the oak tree, God began the conversation in Judges chapter 6.

Then the angel of the LORD came and sat under the oak that was in Ophrah, which belonged to Joash the Abiezrite as his son Gideon was beating

---

1 Model Systems Knowledge Translation Centre MSKTC, *Depression and Spinal Cord Injury*, https://msktc.org/sci/factsheets/depression (Online 2021, January)

out wheat in the wine press in order to save it from the Midianites. The angel of the LORD appeared to him and said to him, "The LORD is with you, O valiant warrior." Then Gideon said to him, "O my lord, if the LORD is with us, why then has all this happened to us? And where are all His miracles which our fathers told us about, saying, 'Did not the LORD bring us up from Egypt?' But now the LORD has abandoned us and given us into the hand of Midian." The LORD looked at him and said, "Go in this your strength and deliver Israel from the hand of Midian." (NASB 1995)

I think it's great that God wasn't even the least bit affected by Gideon's questions or even the tone in which he might have been using when talking with God. It was probably oozing with sarcasm and disbelief. I would imagine he was feeling let down by God and inadvertently saying, "You failed us, God! Why did You let this happen?" Does that sound familiar?

Is there anyone out there who's been told you can't get upset with God or you can't bring your doubts and frustrations to Him? They're sadly mistaken. And again, I apologize if you have not been properly introduced to Him. But let's keep going because it gets better.

Picture it with me: Gideon accepted the challenge to "step up" and lead. The Lord continued to prepare him to face the Midianite army by confirming it was really Him speaking. Gideon sounds the battle call and thousands of Israelites who had previously fled begin to gather. He was looking at his army of 32,000, and guess what God said? "You have too many." And then He gave Gideon instructions which result in reducing his army to 10,000 men. As a side note, the Midianite army outnumbers them with forces too numerous to count! You can imagine how Gideon must have felt as he prepared for battle against the vast Midianite army with only 10,000 of his troops remaining.

But we aren't finished yet. If you know the story, you know where I am going with this, so bear with me. However, if you're hearing this for the first time get ready to be amazed! God tells Gideon he *still* has too many. *What*? Are you kidding me? What is the purpose of this?

God had originally told Gideon, *"You have too many warriors with you. If I let all of you fight the Midianites, the Israelites will boast to me that they saved themselves by their own strength." Judges 7:2 (NLT)* You have to read the whole story for full details which can be found in Judges 6 & 7 or you can also find a small book titled, *Chosen – Conversations of God With His Mighty Warrior,* written by my editor which I've listed in the resources.[2]

But ultimately Gideon's army was reduced from 32,000 men, right down to 300. By now I am sure that Gideon is getting quite fearful again and thinking, "God, I can't - this is impossible!" Can you relate to this story? I know we have all plead with God, "Please let me go back to where it's comfortable." Or maybe you're afraid to step out at all? I hope you're finding some courage from Gideon's story.

Gideon pushes though his fear as God supernaturally gives him a word of encouragement. Then Gideon announces the instructions for battle. Brace yourself because it's about to get to *another* one of my favorite parts. God sends Gideon and the 300 men into battle against the horde of Midianites. However, they are going not armed with swords, but with trumpets, empty jars, and torches. Can you imagine what Gideon must have felt? Or can you imagine what the "pep talk" for that battle must have been like as he stood before the soldiers telling them, "Well guys, here we are down to 300 men and, by the way, each of us will get a trumpet, jar, and torch as weapons."

That was exactly where God wanted them to be: feeling totally outnumbered with no chance of survival in their own strength and *totally dependent on Him!* Gideon and his army surrounded the camp at night. On cue, they smashed their jars containing the lit torches, blew their trumpets, and gave a loud shout.

The Midianite army woke in chaos, started killing each other in their fear and confusion of being under attack, and then Gideon's men chased them out of the land in victorious pursuit.

Remember my trip to Newfoundland Labrador when I was speaking for the first time after my re-commitment to the Lord? Well my sister was there with me and she has been with me through *everything*! In the moments just before we left for the service, I was feeling so insecure and afraid. I felt like a big hypocrite. How I could speak about God's love and strength when I had failed so many times, and I still didn't have it all together! When I told

---

2 Peggy Kennedy, *Chosen – Conversations of God With His Mighty Warrior*, (Guardian Books 2012)

her, she laughed and said, "Vahen, no one wants to hear from someone who's not been through some _____." Honestly, that was my own oak tree experience. I was heading into battle feeling totally outnumbered with no chance of survival in my own strength. Yet her words lifted something off me that day that I can't explain. God used her to give the same message He gave Gideon, "Oh, valiant warrior, the Lord is with you. Go in this your strength."

We rarely think that our strengths could be a hindrance in the work of God. Yet it is harder to rely on God when we feel we are quite capable of completing the task ahead without God's help. My guess is that if I didn't need Him, I *would* most likely attempt many things in my own strength. But the most amazing part is that God calls us in spite of our weakness. He then requires us to *choose* to trust God as Gideon did. The option would be to disobey. Without God fighting with us, we have no chance of victory. Maybe we'll do okay for a while, but the truth is that we can't defeat the giants in our own strength. We will always be limited.

Gideon and his 300 soldiers defeated the Midianite army without having to do anything other than blow trumpets, break jars, yell and then give hot pursuit. That gave way to a dramatic conclusion of this epic victory. If there was a movie review of Gideon's story it would probably be this, "From a state of fear, weakness, and insecurity, Gideon emerged as Israel's hero, filled with God's presence and His passion for deliverance."[3]

I've come to realize that our biggest disabilities or limitations are often the ones we put on ourselves. My newfound freedom or success was not found in highlighting my strengths or "filtered" truths. Rather, I had to embrace my insecurities and weaknesses and only then could I boast about God's strength in me. Gideon's story has all 3 of the elements I mentioned at the start to watch for: faith, obedience and discipline.

Now in this final section of how to live a life of contagious courage I'll be including more stories of how my weakness and physical handicap have become one of my greatest strengths as I have put into practice these 3 key elements. My contagious courage has unlocked a level of freedom I didn't

---

3 Priscilla Shirer, *Gideon - Your Weakness God's Strength,* (Lifeway Press, 2013), Book description
   https://www.goingbeyond.com/resources/workbooks/gideon-member-book/ (2021, January)

know existed. But the truth remains that I am simply a confidently imperfect girl who said yes to God. I pray you will also say yes to God and allow Him to help you understand *The Strength of Your Weakness*.

Chapter 20

A Courageous Prayer of Blessing

Have you ever played that children's game: "If You had 3 Wishes?" The idea is that you can dream about whatever you want and share your 3 wishes with your friends. I remember a time when I was playing this with my childhood friends. I listed off 2 wishes, but then as I thought about my third wish, I said, "I wish that all the wishes I wished would come true." Don't you wish that life was like that? How awesome would it be if we could just ask God for things and He would grant our wishes? What would you ask for?

I remember being out with a friend shopping one day when she randomly asked me, "Vahen, if God were standing in front of you right now and asked you if you wanted to be healed, what would you say?" My jaw hit the ground. With tears in my eyes I said," I would ask Him if that's what *He* wanted for *me*?"

What would it look like for God to show up and *ask you what you wanted*? If all the prayers you have been praying came true, what would your life be like? Would you be driving a better car, have a better job, or finally have __?___. You fill in the blank. Would the world around *you* be better or just *your* world? I can assure you, my wishes and even my prayers over the years were mostly about *my* life being better. Certainly, there's nothing wrong with asking God for a better job, a bigger house, or in my case, a healing. He may very well bless us in these different ways, but what would it mean on an even higher level for God to *bless* us? That has been something I've really been challenged with in my life.

I know God is not this genie-in-a-bottle we can simply approach and get whatever we want. However, when my friend asked me that question, there was another issue at play. This had been a long-standing issue for me. My answer to my friend reflected that I was terrified to ask for the *wrong* thing. You know, for a long time I desired "things" that took me away from God. And it was compounded by feeling I had not received the big long-awaited answer of my healing. So, from where I was sitting (literally—still in my chair) trying not to ask too much from God was better than asking and getting let down. That would only result in my not trusting Him at all.

It's not wrong to desire nice things, it simply more about what I covered in my "What Are You Seeking?" chapter. Did I want God to bless me? Absolutely, but I've gotten sidetracked so many times with the things *I* thought were best for me. Now I wanted to ensure I had "God's best."

Back in 2019, I was invited to speak at the "Woman of Vision" conference in Montreal. The topic was "No Limits," with 1 Chronicles 4:10 as the main focus. It's a short but courageous prayer by a man named Jabez. His request was, *"Oh that you would bless me, expand my territory, be with me in all that I do, and keep me safe" And God granted him his request." (NLT)*

Why do we consider Jabez's words as a courageous prayer when he asked God to bless him? Maybe you actually see that as a selfish prayer and not a courageous one? If all we are asking for is a bigger car or a better house—maybe you're right. Before I understood what "blessing" meant, I felt that way as well. So here I was, developing a full weekend around this concept of God blessing us from this little prayer. I dusted off the cover of my "Prayer Of Jabez" book. And when I started looking into what *"blessing"* means, it really opened my eyes. I realized that I had actually prayed this prayer long before I understood it.

That bold prayer I prayed my first year of Bible College seems to keep popping up. I had said, "God, I'll go through anything as long as I know You're with me." I didn't realize it then, but my prayer was very similar to what Jabez prayed. I didn't pray for a life without pain, I was praying for Him to be with me in whatever I was going to face. I wanted my life to be a blessing. Unknowingly, I wanted God to bless me in His timing and according to *His* will, not *mine*.

As that young, vibrant Bible College student there was no way I could have imagined what was ahead of me. In all of the plans I had envisioned for my life of "blessing," or in all the things I could have asked for, being struck with a paralyzing virus that contributed to my detour onto a destructive path was not ever considered. And, when that destructive path lead to infidelity and living a life without hope, I had strayed far from my original vision of "blessing."

In those dark hours I often questioned everything: "I have loved God my whole life and yet there I was, right smack in the middle of some of the biggest challenges of my life! *This was not fair!" I didn't understand why* this was happening to me.

Many times as I reflected on that college prayer, I thought maybe what God heard instead was: *"Oh God, curse me! Limit me in all I do, lead me right through danger and allow me to suffer physical, emotional and spiritual brokenness. And oh, by the way, I don't need your protection."* If you are wondering how I could ever make that faulty assumption, I simply was looking in the rear-view mirror at the last several chapters of my life! But, my mistake was looking through a faulty lenses.

I don't want you to think God causes us pain and suffering, but I want to acknowledge that He did allow it. And if I am being completely honest, there's actually a lot of room for celebration! My pain journey has indeed been a blessing that has enabled me to live a life of overflow, with the ability to be a blessing to others in ways I never thought possible.

I keep being drawn back to what my sister said to me before I spoke that one time. She said, "Vahen, no one wants to listen to someone who's not been through some __?__." While you know that this journey nearly destroyed me, I can tell you emphatically that I would rather be on this side with all my scars and a life story to encourage you, than to have lived a life without any understanding of what you might be going through. You might not be on the other side yet and that's okay; it took me *forever*. But I can say with confidence the words of James 1:2-4, *"I consider it pure joy, because I have faced these trials, because I know that the testing of my faith produced perseverance. I've let perseverance finish its work so that I can be mature and complete, not lacking anything." (NIV)*

There are so many ways to be a blessing and it's not only as a result of pain. You can bless someone by paying for a stranger's coffee at a drive-thru. It could mean you babysit for a single mom who needs a night to herself. Blessing someone could be as simple as saying thank you to someone who did something without expecting anything in return. The list is endless for the way others can bless or be a blessing. If you're saying, "No one ever blesses *me,*" why not look for a way to bless someone else.

Ironically enough, before I sat at my computer today to fine tune this chapter about blessings, I was enjoying my time with the Lord as is my morning routine. I was surprised and delighted to see the heading "Be a Blessing" in my daily reading! I pulled out this little nugget to share with you: *"The beautiful thing about being a blessing is that people respond to the light you are giving off. They may not even realize that you are pointing them straight to Jesus. What better reason to be a blessing!"*[1] Wouldn't it be a blessing to have peace when there is nothing but chaos surrounding you? People would see that unexplainable peace and wonder how they can get it. We can ask God to remove our pain, but what about God giving us strength *in* that pain? What about having defiant joy? Defiant joy I assure you is a strength like nothing I've ever experienced. That kind of inner blessing *is contagious.* When I began to view my suffering and unwelcome circumstances through a different lens, I began to see blessings beyond anything I could ever have imagined!

Bless Me

I was in Banff, AB for a week-long pastors' conference. While I always love these conferences, I went there on the heels of the Hope Conference. So, by the time the week was over, I was looking forward to getting home. Despite the fellowship and the great messages, I was feeling mentally and physically exhausted. However, I still needed to drive four hours to reach my home in Edmonton, AB.

---

1 April Rodgers, *Made To Shine: Enjoy & Reflect God's Light*, A 10 Day Devotional, (DaySprings, YouVersion Bible App), Day 2 of 10

As my friend and I were leaving to put our suitcases in the car, I was praying, "God, give me the strength to drive home." The elevator doors opened and within seconds my friend said, "Vahen, you have a flat tire!" I fought against the urge to cry. We had just heard a message titled "Praise Him in the Storm." In almost a joking tone but desperate to find the strength to get through the task ahead, I let out a "Hallelujah! Praise the Lord anyway!"

The hotel staff were great, we discovered that my main tire had a screw in it and they were able to install my mini spare tire for me. Unfortunately they strongly recommended I should not drive 4 hours on the mini spare tire. So that meant I would need to get a new tire before I headed home. Other friends who were also leaving for the day were also trying to help me figure out where to go. And honestly, at this point I didn't know how to process what I was feeling. I mean I was *seriously* considering driving home on that spare. So, to just have that additional support was so needed and valued.

We found a repair shop in a nearby town, but they were all booked until the following day! However, after much pleading on my part about needing to get home *today*, the gentleman said that they would try to get me in after lunch.

I looked at the time and it was 12:30 p.m. I thought, "That's only an hour or so to wait. By the time we have lunch surely my tire will be ready and we can get on the road."

On our way to lunch I said to my friend, "Well, here we are in Canmore. I wonder what assignment God has for us?"

We had our lunch. It was now 1:10 p.m. I thought I'd call to get some idea about when my car would get through the shop. I was assured that although they hadn't started yet, I'd be next in line!

As we were waiting at the nearby coffee shop, we saw two older gentlemen and started a conversation with them. That conversation turned out to be pretty amazing. It was what you would call a "divine appointment." As we talked, we knew that they needed the encouragement being shared. We were so caught up in conversation that I didn't even realize how quickly the time was flying by. It was now 2:30 p.m., and I still hadn't received a call back about my car.

One of the gentlemen said, "This is taking way too long," and offered to go and find out what the delay was. I said, "Oh no, but thank you." I didn't want to cause trouble with the shop since they were already doing us the favor of fitting us in unscheduled. Although still unsure, I said, "Let's wait until 3:00 p.m. to see if I hear anything." Well, when 3:00 p.m. came I gave the shop another call. This time I couldn't even get through to see how long it would be! Again the kind gentleman offered to go find out what was happening. So, I agreed to let our new friends go see what was taking so long.

When he returned, he said, "I have good news and bad news. I'll give you the bad news first. Your car isn't in the shop yet, and from the sounds of it, probably won't be in at all today. The good news is, I called the Ford dealership because I work there, and they agreed to take you *now*!"

Long story short, we were welcomed and treated like family as we waited at the Ford dealership. The conversations and interaction with the staff just made this flat tire fiasco become more of a blessing than we could have even imagined! We got to meet all the staff at Cam Clark Ford in Canmore and even our new friend's teenage daughter.

With each delay came a new perspective on the *assignment* we were on. Then as we were discussing the repair details, the manager came over and told the sales rep, "Now if you don't give this lady 50% off, I'll be *very* upset with you!

I had tears! He had tears! It was a beautiful moment as I tried to express my gratitude.

Then when the sales rep came with my bill, he said, "I'm not giving you 50% off, because I'm not charging you *at all*." Well, I started crying again, and I said, "You *know* this is not about the money, right?" With tears in my eyes, I looked around and saw the other staff all standing around with tears in their eyes. I continued, "This is not about the money and would you like to know why? God keeps reminding me, "Vahen, I am taking care of you." He keeps challenging me to trust Him all the time. And today, God used my flat tire and all of you, my new friends, to show me that no matter what, He's *got me*!"

There I was in the Ford showroom telling the staff and managers about the love of Jesus. When it was time to go, the manager said, "Wow, you have no idea how you've blessed us today." We left that day knowing there were seeds of love planted.

The next morning, I posted a *glowing* review on the Cam Clark Ford social media page and this was the response I received: *"Thank you, Vahen, for the kinds words! We are so grateful to serve you and your smile. Your positive outlook was contagious through the dealership. And all our staff left work with a smile on their face! Look forward to seeing you again."*

I wonder what blessings (and divine appointments!) we are missing out on every day because we can't see past the frustration or pain to see the true blessing.

Was it a blessing to end up in a wheelchair? No! Was it a blessing to have a flat tire or be stranded? No! And it's even okay to say, this is not okay. It's okay to say, "God, I don't want this pain journey." It's okay to say, "God, if there is another way, please let me have that way."

Do you know why I know that? Because in the hours before Jesus died for you and me, He said the same thing? He was in the garden praying and cried so much He literally sweat blood. Luke 22:42, tells us that He said, *"Father, if you are willing, please take this cup of suffering away from me. Yet, I want your will to be done, not mine." (NLT)* That's a hard prayer to pray, isn't it? Yet, Jesus' pain and suffering were necessary for our freedom. And Hebrews 5:8 tells us that, *"Though He was God's Son, he learned trusting-obedience by what he suffered, just as we do." (MSG)*

Our pain, which can be nearly unbearable, holds the potential for us to grow and experience true blessings in our lives. When I am willing to accept these perceived negative experiences in my life and give them to God, He is able to use them to speak encouragement into someone else's life. He is still using the surrender of my disability to help others find a path forward. But it wasn't until I surrendered my will and *what I could see*, that I could *truly* see what He sees! Only then was I able to catch a glimpse of the bigger blessing.

How many would say you feel cursed instead of blessed? Is there something that's holding you back and limiting your freedom? Maybe it's not physical. Maybe it's shame about your past. Maybe it's depression, or a broken relationship, or self-doubt? No matter what it is, the enemy wants to limit you with your pain and all the negative fall-out. But God has a totally different plan. He wants you to be free — to make you a blessing in spite of your pain.

When I talk about growing through what you go through, I don't say that lightly. Walking through the pain to get to restoration is hard. Dealing with the loss of my independence was excruciating. But, receiving the blessing of knowing true dependency on God's strength and not my own, is a blessing like nothing I have ever asked for. This has expanded my territory farther than I could have ever dreamed. My life is not void of pain, but I have learned to trust God in my pain. As a result, I have unexplainable peace, defiant joy, with more opportunities to encourage others with my contagious courage than I ever thought possible!

When things don't go as we planned, when people don't treat us as we think we should be treated, or when our "wishes/prayers" aren't answered as we hoped, we need to have courage daily to fight against pride, anger, and our need for control. While God didn't cause these situations, you can be sure that once you surrender to Him, He will use them to build up your faith and your character! Or He may use you to encourage someone else or build their faith!

Are you ready to move forward into receiving God's intended blessings for your life? Are you ready to surrender your will today and pray this courageous prayer: *"God, I want You to bless me, in Your timing, and according to Your will, not mine."* When you allow God to work in you, he will bless you and expand your territory so that He can do tremendous things through you! If you have the opportunity for your life to exemplify those kinds of blessings, wouldn't you want to ask for that?

I am reminded of the words of Ephesians 3:20 in which the Lord is said to be able to do way more than we can ever ask or think. Thank you for joining me in the adventure of discovering the blessings of praying a courageous prayer.

Now, allow me to declare Colossians 1:9, over you. *"...I ask God to give you complete knowledge of his will and to give you spiritual wisdom and understanding. Then the way you live will always honor and please the Lord.*

I pray that your lives will produce every kind of good fruit. I pray that you grow as you learn to know God better and better. I also pray that you will be strengthened with all his glorious power so you will have all the endurance and patience you need. May you be filled with joy." (NLT)

Chapter 21

Igniting Hearts With Hope

There have been some very amazing incremental steps to where the Lord has now opened many doors for me to share my message of hope. Allow me to take you back to 2017 when my friend asked if I wanted to go to Vancouver to enter the first-ever Miss Wheelchair Canada pageant. That was a step that I definitely had to take by faith. In fact, I almost didn't! My first response to that request was "NO!" I wondered if this was really for me. Plus, I was only a few months away from becoming an ordained minister. Let me just stop here for a moment and laugh with you, but also acknowledge that our plans for what *we* think is best are often so different than what God has planned. God's plans are not only *different*, but so much *better*. My thoughts were, "Is this really something a gal in her 40's about to become a "reverend" should be doing?"

While I had some people close to me acknowledge that it would be a great opportunity to have a "voice," I didn't want to be on any platform without God's approval. So I prayed, "Okay, God, if this is a door you are opening for me, then my husband and my family need to approve. Plus, even though I can afford to go, if you make a way so my expenses are covered, I'll *know* it's you." And, for good measure, I added, "Oh, and by the way, I won't be asking anyone for the money."

I talked it over with my husband. While he laughed and said pageants really weren't his thing, he would support me if I felt to go. I was shocked that he was so compliant and didn't even mention the finances. But I still wasn't convinced. Then came time to tell my parents. I thought for sure they would tell me, "Vahen, get real, you're a grown woman." (Or something like that.) But on the contrary, my mom said, "Vahen, I wouldn't discount it. Maybe

God will use this to give you a 'voice.'" By this time, I was definitely starting to think God *was* opening this door. I was beginning to see that maybe He was going to use my wheelchair as a platform of hope. But I still had to find accommodations *and* "get there."

While I was talking with my friend who had informed me about the pageant (and who, by the way, was also travelling to Vancouver) I mentioned that I didn't know where I would stay. Her response was, "I have relatives there. You can stay with us." I was shocked by how fast things were coming together. But I still had to "get there," so I was not 100% convinced.

That evening I went out for dinner with two friends. I told them about this opportunity, but I did not tell them about my prayer and my "conditions". When I finished telling them, my one friend's next words were, "I have extra travel points and would love to help. Can I take care of your flight?" It was at *that* point I broke down and cried. The only response I could give was, "Well, I guess I'm going to the first-ever Miss Wheelchair Canada pageant." I then told them about my prayer conditions. Soon we were all in tears.

By opening this door for me, God made it really clear that this was indeed an amazing opportunity for my wheelchair to be a platform of hope for others. I had ample confirmation that His purpose was to expand my sphere of influence and have an amazing experience in the process. However, because I prayed and asked God to make it clear, I knew it wasn't me simply making it happen. He was making it happen.

There's another detail I need to share before I move on. In the midst of all the planning my husband surprised me and said, "Would you mind if I came with you?" Isn't God amazing! So, off to Vancouver I went, with hubby at my side, to compete in the first-ever Miss Wheelchair Canada pageant. We were able to stay with relatives that I had totally forgotten lived near there!

Two weeks after I had won Miss Wheelchair Canada, I was on the world stage in Poland representing Canada in the Miss Wheelchair World pageant. Again, with the support of *many,* all expenses were covered for that trip, too. Then the fact that my sister was able to be my travel buddy was another blessing that to this day meant so much to me. We will always treasure this "sisters' experience."

1

Through this part of *my* history, God used that platform to achieve the title of Miss Kindness World. The competition plus the title was another way He provided even more opportunities for my future. Let me share a quote from the Miss Wheelchair World organizers when winning the title Miss Kindness World. *"We gave the finalists an opportunity to become the judge. They were granted the ability to vote for the most friendly, kind-hearted and favorable of them all. The title Miss Kindness has been awarded to Vahen King from Canada! Congratulations Vahen King."*

I wasn't at all disappointed I didn't win the title of *Miss Wheelchair World* since Canada is considered a nation of kindness. This title was truly a great honour and blessing. And as a result, I have been featured on many different media outlets and platforms spreading my message of hope and courage.

I have also had the honour of having some of my words of inspiration translated into two other languages. One article was from a connection I made in Poland. He is the president of a networking club for the businesswomen of Poland. He asked me to write a few words of inspiration which would be translated into Polish. My story would then be included in an international

---

1 Photo: Credit: Dawid Fuz - Instagram @13w13

publication featuring the top 70 businesswomen and entrepreneurs of 2017. Another article I wrote was translated into Russian and was distributed to over 36 Russian-speaking countries.

The Lord was true to His word. That step into the pageant world did indeed open many doors and give me a voice to ignite hearts with hope. In 2019, I was honoured to have been nominated for the Marilyn Snyder award. This is one of Alberta's Premier's Council awards. It is an award given to acknowledge someone who has not let their physical disability limit their personal or professional success. That same year I was also featured at International Day for Persons with Disabilities by Easter Seals Alberta as someone who is making a difference in their community.

The experiences I've had as a result of conquering my fears have been incredible. The blessings just keep coming; and yet, I have not even told you the *best part*. You see people look at the "highlights reel" of my life with all the external blessing and say, "Wow, you are so blessed." I respond and say, "You are correct. I am blessed. But that's simply the "fruit" of the biggest blessings: unexplainable peace, defiant joy, and contagious courage. My biggest blessings are only possible because of the amazing God I serve. He enables me to ignite hearts with hope on my most valued platform— everywhere I set my foot.

I have story after story of the "blessings received" from my contagious courage, simply as a result of saying, "God, not my will, but Yours." Blessings that are the result of my faith to keep going when I couldn't understand. Blessings as a result of my unreserved obedience. Blessings as a result of the discipline to keep God close and not quit. These stories of blessings are not about a bigger house or better job. They are not even about the crown or all the titles. Rather, these incredible stories of blessings are the fruit of my God-given contagious courage. Please allow me to share a few more stories that have been shared with me throughout my journey of using my freedom and courage to bless others.

The first one is from a struggling wife/mother. "*I am so impressed with your transparency in your book Going Farther. I just finished reading your chapter about the infidelity and am encouraged that things do get better after this has happened. My husband is cheating. But it's really great to hear the other side. It's been 5 years, and we are still struggling with communication and everything else in a marriage, especially intimacy. It's still so hard and something that only God can fully heal. I have my son, and he is what keeps me going. I just keep praying that my marriage one day will be fully restored and healed. It's so hard! Thank you for sharing your story, please keep me in your prayers."*

This next story is from a husband who said, *"I just wanted to send a note saying how much I appreciate your book. I must admit I have been in tears most of the time reading it. My life has been an absolute and total mess for so many years and I have been so filled with hurt, anger and bitterness. I too have felt that God could no longer love me. All I can say right now is thank you for your openness in writing this book. Maybe God can still use me yet"*

On one of my travels I received this message from a young adult in her early 20's who said, *"Vahen because of your courage to talk about your weakness, I felt safe to come forward and tell you that I have been battling thoughts of suicide. Until today, I've never had the courage to tell anyone."* That became the day she had the courage to connect with a counsellor and seek out the help she needed.

Another trip, while I was concluding a message I literally felt God was wanting me to make a plea to the audience on behalf of the "broken" who were maybe too afraid to speak for themselves. With tears rolling down my face, I passionately gave voice to what might have been the silent plea of those in the room. "I'm struggling with pornography; will you help me?" "I have an addiction and I'm afraid to tell anyone because I'm a Christian." As I spoke out each different plea of desperation, I pointed randomly to individuals in the crowd as if I were begging them for help. I could feel the intensity of God's presence in the room. I knew He wanted to meet people right where they were. I asked, "What if there are people here now in this room struggling, but they are afraid to ask for help? Are we that "safe place?" Can we love people where they are without judgment?"

When I gave the invitation to receive Christ that night, 7 people responded. Six of them were young teenagers. Another lady approached me and thanked me for being so real. She continued, *"You see, I am trying to be a Christian, but I am addicted to drugs. And I used to sell my body for money. Now, I'm afraid I'll be alone for the rest of my life—afraid that no one will love trash like me."*

Oh, God, that you would bless me! Expand my territory! The prayer of Jabez continues to take on very practical meaning for me for the sake of so many! God continues to show us that real blessings are to be a blessing and to *ignite hearts with hope.* To rise and shine.

Chapter 22

Rise and Shine

1

On January 1, 2020, I woke up from a very vivid dream. In it I was being taught to make bread from scratch. It looked something like when I was in Uganda and the ladies were showing me how *they* made bread. I remembered laughing because I said, "My strategy is always quick and easy, and with the fewest steps possible." But there I was in the dream being taught to make bread from scratch and feeling pretty good about myself. I had all the ingredients and the determination to try, so I was good to go. However, the next thing I knew the bread was coming out of the oven, but it was flat. I was so confused. I said, "But I had all of the ingredients, what went wrong? Why didn't my bread rise?"

In my dream there was an older gentleman watching. He came over and said, "Yes, Vahen, you *had* all the ingredients, but *look,* you forgot to add the key ingredient. You forgot the yeast." My heart sank. Feeling quite embarrassed, I yelled! "OH NO! How could I forget the yeast? I made sure I had everything I needed. How did I make this mistake?"

I was trying to rationalize my blunder by emphasizing how nervous I'd been about making the bread from scratch. In my excitement I got sidetracked. But whatever the reason, nothing would change the fact: I forgot the yeast.

---

1 Lance King, *Turtle on a Post,* Image credit

The dream continued as the older gentleman was then compelled to give me some spiritual insight. He said, "Vahen, just like yeast is the key ingredient to cause your bread to rise, prayer is the key ingredient that God uses to help *you* rise. Don't let anything distract you from focusing on the task at hand." He continued with this: "The way you used to do things before, even your former mindset, will not be enough when you're creating something from scratch."

I understood that dream as God's way of reminding me to be diligent with all the things He has blessed me with. And, even more importantly, He was providing a word of caution by reminding me to stay focused and not get distracted. Those words about prayer as the *priority* ingredient lingered as a powerful reminder to keep it as that "must-have" ingredient. What a vivid illustration that I can't *rise* or "rise above" without Him. And, He really is calling us all to "rise *and* shine!"

This message certainly spoke volumes to me at the beginning of 2020. Later, as the unforeseen Covid-19 global events rolled out, this message was screaming. Now more than ever, it is important to make prayer our priority. If we don't, we will fall flat and not rise as God intends.

If you ask me about my journey of being a person with a disability, I will tell you that it's not always been easy. However, I am going farther emotionally, spiritually, and physically than I ever thought possible. We've already celebrated together how the courage to face my fears and keep pushing forward has led me to some of the most amazing experiences and into the fulfilment of my wildest dreams.

As a result of keeping prayer as that key ingredient in my life, God has been increasingly using my story of hope and courage to create a large ripple effect. That "reach" has resulted in being able to influence and impact people from all over the world. The popularity and the capability of global digital communication has facilitated that increase.

Back to 2014. I was invited by a friend to attend "Western Canadian Fashion Week" here in Edmonton, Alberta. (Ironically, it was the same girl who would tell me three years later about the Miss Wheelchair Canada pageant.) To close out every show at "Fashion Week" event, the emcee called upon the audience for volunteers to do their best runway walk. The reward was that they would win some free product.

When I first heard that announcement, my heart started pounding. I really wanted to go, but thought, "I can't do that, can I? I mean, I'm in a wheelchair. I'll probably look funny up there." When no one else jumped up at the first call, I thought maybe I would have a chance since no one else had volunteered. So, when the second call was given, I quickly raised my hand and said, "I will." The emcee looked at me with her eyes and mouth wide open in surprise, "You can do that?" "I sure can!" was my bold response.

Without hesitation two of my friends lifted me onto the runway and I just went for it. I was fully committed to the experience and held nothing back. I thought, "If I've learned anything at all from Tyra Banks on "America's Top Model" it was to smile from H2T (head to toe.)" So, smiling with my whole body, down the runway I went. Making eye contact with the cheering crowds along the way gave me such a boost of confidence. I even did a little twirl midway down the runway in my wheelchair. (You can find this video on

my YouTube channel by searching for Vahen King "Western Canada Fashion Week.")

Then, upon reaching the end of the runway, I gave my best "Look at me, I'm beautiful" pose. Hearing the crowd and seeing the flashing cameras, I thought "Wow, that's all for me?"

But do you want to know the best part? While I was definitely shining on that raised platform, the brightest moment was what happened after my catwalk experience.

When I got down off the runway, my friend who was with

Image credit: https://www.tracygrabowskiphoto.com

me who was recently paralyzed and also in a wheelchair said, "Vahen, last night when I was here and the emcee made the same request to the audience, she pointed to me, not knowing I was in this chair. She said, "What about you?" Feeling so embarrassed, I hung my head and in front of everyone

said, "I can't, I'm in a wheelchair." So when you got up there tonight on that runway without a second thought, I said," Wow, look at her go! I wish I had her confidence."

You want to know another amazing dimension to this whole story? This same girl who said, "I wish I had your confidence," was the same girl I had the privilege of passing on the crown to in 2018—four years after saying she didn't have the confidence to rise and shine! What an incredible shared moment as she was crowned the 2nd Miss Wheelchair Canada. And this beauty sitting beside me is not only the reigning Miss Wheelchair Canada, but she also now runs her own rehabilitation facility here in Edmonton, Alberta.[1]

Her determination for her health and overall fitness is something that God uses even today to challenge and encourage me to be better and to keep trying. Even as I worked on this chapter, I saw her post an amazing workout video. She was showing how she is now doing squats without holding on to bars. That video motivated me get up and start exercising on the spot.

When you see that your courage has the power to inspire others to choose courage, then that is a whole new way to live. Now her courage is also inspiring me!

As a teenager I would always repeat the phrase: "Keep God in the centre of everything, and everything will come together." Prayer for me means I'm

---

1 Reyu Paralysis Recovery Centre

daily keeping Him in the centre. That is the one key element that enables me to walk by faith when I can't see and to be obedient to God over the fear of man or my own insecurities. It's the ingredient that keeps me disciplined to keep going and not fall flat on my face. I know there is no perfect recipe for how to handle all that life throws at you, but I have taken you back through my journey to show that " process." I trust that you will find the strength to begin or to continue yours.

Remember the image of the turtle sitting on the fencepost at the beginning of the chapter? There's only one way it could have gotten there. So, when you see me elevated on *any* platform, whether it's a runway, a pageant stage, a school gymnasium, TV or any media outlet, just know I didn't get there on my own. I have learned to surrender to the One who enables me to *rise and shine.*

To know that it's God who has elevated me to *be* a blessing is the biggest blessing I could ask for. Allow me to remind you about those important instructions from my dream: "Don't let anything distract you from focusing on the task at hand." Prayer is the priority, and while it's great to embrace the inspiration of others, the key ingredient for me is truly prayer.

Get ready! The flame from your elevated platform will indeed be contagious—igniting hope in someone's heart. I pray that you too will experience what it means to *Rise and Shine!*

Reflect & Review

One More Step

I don't want to wait on the sidelines.
I don't want to waste my time.
Looking back, wishing that, I'd done it differently.
Why do I carry burdens that aren't mine?
Walk around pretending I'm fine.

And in vain, I hold the chains, that no one else can see.
Always thinking I can earn your love but I can't, no I can't.
And yet there's nothing I could do that will make it go.

So I put one foot in front of the other.
Keep walking, keep walking.
Each day a little bit farther.
Just keep walking, keep walking.
One more step, don't turn back around.[1]

---

1 One More Step. Written and performed by Kelly Marie Elford. © (2015)

Chapter 23

Your Courage Assessment

Congratulations for making it this far! You might be feeling any number of things right now, and I want you to know that I understand that this journey to freedom in any area of your life is difficult. Some of you might even be feeling things for the very first time and not know how to process what you are feeling or know where to begin.

After hosting my Night of Courage event in November of 2020, I had someone send me this message: *"After watching night of courage my spirit is wrestling. I'm feeling I need to do something, but I don't know what to do or how to do it. I am also wrestling fear, excitement and awe. Praying I can make sense of everything I am feeling, so I can know what I need to do."*

I don't know a better way to say it than that. In reading this book you've seen my journey and perhaps you feel overwhelmed and don't know where to begin. Maybe *something* has been ignited, but you either don't know what to do, or are afraid to take that first step. This section is here to assist you in separating and *reflecting* on what you have just experienced.

So, let's go section by section and reflect and review some areas that maybe you weren't able to address before. Let's acknowledge them now and return when you are ready. There is a well-known phrase you may have heard which says "That which is measured improves. That which is measured and reported improves exponentially."[1] When you write down your starting measurements, you can set your goals. Then when you look back you can see how far you've grown. Remember: change happens one step at a time and one choice at a time.

---

1 Karl Pearson: Quote, www.azquotes.com/quote/727622 (Online 2021, January)

Section 1: Courage IS Possible

1. What area(s) are you struggling with that may be causing you to not know where to begin? And remember; *"My grace is sufficient for you, for my power is made perfect in weakness. Therefore, I will boast all the more gladly about my weaknesses, so that Christ's power may rest on me."* *2 Corinthians 12:9 (NIV)*

_____

_____

_____

_____

_____

_____

2. James R. Sherman says, "Though no one can go back and make a brand-new start, anyone can start from now and make a brand-new ending."[2] Is there something that you would like God to do a Ctrl-Z on?

_____

_____

_____

_____

_____

_____

---

2 James R. Sherman, *Rejection*, (Published by Pathway Books, Golden Valley, Minnesota. 1982), 35.

3. Are you living like the big iceberg—afraid of what people will think if they saw the mess that is underneath? (Answer yes or no) _____ If yes, write down what you are afraid to show about yourself, and why?

_____

_____

_____

_____

_____

_____

4. "There are no shortcuts to healing, no magic solution. However, when God gets in the middle of life's mess, bad becomes good."[3] Genesis 50:20 tells us that what was meant for "bad" God will use for "good." My creative summary of what God was saying; "Let me recycle that pain. Let me create something beautiful." In order for God to recycle our pain we need to give it to Him. Is there any pain that you are hanging onto that you need to let go of?

_____

_____

_____

_____

_____

_____

3 Max Lucado, *God Will Carry You Through, Ultimate Victory,* YouVersion devotional, Day 8

5. Trying to understand where all your "pieces" fit is indeed a steep learning curve. Especially when you know that life will always be filled with pain or unwelcomed circumstances. Are there any pieces of your life that just don't seem to fit right now? If so, write them down. And then, I challenge you to see God's perspective on your puzzle pieces and allow Him to give you the courage to lean on His strength and power as you trust Him to create something beautiful.

Section 2: Preparing for a Life of Courage

1. In chapter 5, what score did you give yourself on the courageous scale when you first read the question: **Are you courageous?** _____ Are you able to give yourself a higher number after understanding what courage is? Can you explain why you changed your answer? Don't forget: "Courage isn't about not being afraid; rather it is about not letting fear control you!"[4] Say it with me, "*I am courageous!*"

----

4 Bruce Wilkinson, *The Dream Giver: Following Your God Given Destiny,* (Multnomah Publishers Sisters, Oregon 2003), 93.

2. If *knowing* is half the battle, how prepared are you for your life of freedom you are wanting to live? What would be a "next step" now that you *know?*

_____

_____

_____

_____

_____

_____

3. If for some reason you still don't believe that courage and freedom are for you, I want to ask you, who's telling you these lies? And why are you believing them? What is one lie you are believing about yourself that you will try to reject today?

_____

_____

_____

_____

_____

_____

4. Do you believe that God loves you and that you are forgiven? Do you believe He has great plans for you and that you *are* worthy? This next question is plain and simple, but not so easy. What IS stopping you from believing this truth?

_____

_____

_____

_____

_____

_____

Section 3: Courage To Grow

1. When I get overwhelmed, I tend to shut down and get stuck. But when I start looking at each day individually and asking myself, "How can I win *today*?" it really helps me feel productive. Stress is greatly reduced. So, what would it look like for you to "win the day?" Would it be planning and enjoying all 3 meals for today? Would it be doing that load of laundry? What can you do today that will help you win today?

A note to remember, "This is why change can be so difficult. Change is always emotional. You have to decide, very intentionally, who you are going to be every single day."[5]

_____

_____

_____

_____

_____

_____

2. Is there something in your *past* that was painful or unbearable, but now as you look back and reflect on it, you see how you grew as a result of what you went through? And what can you take away from that experience that can help you in your *current* situation?

_____

_____

_____

_____

_____

_____

---

5 This Morning Routine Will Make You Unstoppable, Benjamin Hardy, PhD
https://medium.com/thrive-global (Online 2021, January)

Some nuggets of truth to remember as you grow:

"Wait patiently for the Lord. Be brave and courageous. Yes, wait patiently for the Lord." Psalms 27:14 (NLT)

"The Lord makes firm the steps of the one who delights in him; though he may stumble, he will not fall, for the Lord upholds him with his hand." Psalms 37:23-24 (NIV)

John 15:5 tells us that *"I am the vine; you are the branches. If you remain in me and I in you, you will bear much fruit; apart from me you can do nothing." (NIV)*

3. Psalm 34: 8 says, *"Taste and see that the Lord is good..." (NIV)* When people are in your presence, do they leave with a good feeling? Or, do they taste the bitterness of unforgiveness or judgment that you carry in your heart?

_____

_____

_____

_____

_____

4. What does your fruit taste like?

0 ----- 1 ----- 2 ----- 3 ----- 4 ----- 5 ----- 6 ----- 7 ----- 8 ----- 9 ----- 10

No one wants to eat my fruit.	I have the seed, but the soil of my heart still needs to be softened.	Bitter to taste but I'm grow-ing	My fruit is ripe and tastes sweet

Comic Title: False Christian Humility   SearchingforGrace.com © Mick Mooney

Section 4: The Cost of Courage

1. *"For all of us who know the amazing (yet demanding) privilege of partnering with our God, the stakes are high! Let us allow His Spirit to sharpen our capacity to receive and respond to revelation. He is fine-tuning all of us to receive what the Spirit is revealing. When we hear His voice calling us to come up higher, will we obey? It will be said of us that we have done what He desires, when we embrace His ways above our own."*[7] In your quest for courage and freedom, or going "higher," is there anything you need to let go of? But more importantly, what are you seeking that might be holding you back?

_____

_____

_____

_____

_____

_____

"Seek ye first the kingdom of God, and his righteousness; and all these things shall be added unto you." Matthew 6:33 (KJV)

6 Mick Mooney, *False Christian Humility Cartoon*, SearchingforGrace.com

7 Peggy Kennedy, *Hear The Sound*, (Newsletter July 1, 2016) http://www.twosilvertrumpets.ca/

2. Matthew 5:6 says, "Blessed are those who hunger and thirst for righteousness, for they will be satisfied." *(NASB)* When you hunger for God, you will run to Him and you will never be left empty. Where you run to for your comfort will determine how much you still have to sacrifice for your courage. What is your muster point? Where do you run when you are afraid? Is it helping?

_____

_____

_____

_____

_____

3. Do you feel off-balance or out of step in some area? When you're walking with someone and you try and keep in step with them, what are some very practical things you would need to do? List them here.

_____

_____

_____

_____

_____

_____

4. How do you think these things can help you as you try to keep in step with God?

_____

_____

_____

_____

_____

I hope my paraphrase of Proverbs 3:5 will provide additional clarity. *"When you trust in the Lord with all your heart and not on your own understanding and you acknowledge Him in all your ways, He will direct your path."*

5. On a scale of 1-10, how much are you willing to surrender for your freedom?

0 ----- 1 ----- 2 ----- 3 ----- 4 ----- 5 ----- 6 ----- 7 ----- 8 ----- 9 ----- 10

Section 5: A Courageous Perspective

1. Are you stuck behind a situation or emotional response that blocks you from moving forward? If so, what do you have to lose or what would you gain by deciding to find another way?

_____

_____

_____

_____

_____

_____

For God has not given us a spirit of fear, but of power and of love and of a sound mind. 2 Timothy 1:7 (NKJV)

2. Do you see how saying, "I can't" stops you before you even begin? Joshua 1:9 tells us "Be strong and courageous!" *(NIV)* Psalm 139:14 tells us, *"That we are fearfully and wonderfully made,"* (NKJV) and that we are loved. Nothing is more powerful than having the God of all the universe tell you that you are loved and wonderfully created! Why do you find it so hard to believe that God wants to do extraordinary things for you and through you?

_____

_____

_____

_____

_____

_____

3. In chapter 17 I covered 3 areas: your view of self, your circumstances, and your view of God. I would like for you to look back at the "lies" vs" truth" chart in chapter 17, and ask yourself. Is there any area in which you need a reboot? If so, what do you think is your biggest obstacle blocking your reboot? (For additional reflect and review, I would suggest going back and reading about Elisha's experience with his servant found in 2 Kings 6:8-23)

_____

_____

_____

_____

_____

_____

4. "'For I know the plans I have for you,' says the LORD. 'They are plans for good and not for disaster, to give you a future and a hope.'" Jeremiah 29:11 (NLT) How would your life be different if your *new normal* would be to adopt the mindset that God has good plans for you and that He wants to prosper you?

_____

_____

_____

_____

_____

_____

Section 6: Living a Life of Contagious Courage

1. In what ways did you relate to Gideon in chapter 19? What weakness do you have that you have been trying to hide?

_____

_____

_____

_____

_____

(a) Why do you believe you want to hide it? And from whom?

_____

_____

_____

_____

_____

_____

(b) (Insert your name on the blank lines) _____ *"The Lord is with you, O valiant warrior."* "From a state of fear, weakness, and insecurity _____ emerges as a hero, filled with God's presence and His passion for deliverance."[8] Again for additional reflection and review, I would suggest going back and reading the whole story of Gideon found in Judges 6 & 7 or consider getting the book *Chosen – Conversations of God With His Mighty Warrior,* written by my editor which I've listed in the resources.[9]

---

8 Priscilla Shirer, *Gideon - Your Weakness God's Strength,* (Lifeway Press, 2013), Book description https://www.goingbeyond.com/resources/workbooks/gideon-member-book/ (Online 2021, January)

9 Peggy Kennedy, *Chosen – Conversations of God With His Mighty Warrior,* (Guardian Books 2012)

2. Remember that short but courageous prayer by a man named Jabez in 1 Chronicles 4:10? *"Oh that you would bless me, expand my territory, be with me in all that I do, and keep me safe" And God granted him his request."* *(NLT)* Whether you've never prayed or you've been praying for decades, I want to ask you: "What would your life look like if all your prayers were answered?

_____

_____

_____

_____

_____

_____

(a) What would you consider a true blessing? Take time to list the top 5 blessings you have in your life.

1. _____

2. _____

3. _____

4. _____

5. _____

(b) And what can you do today to be a blessing to someone else?

_____

_____

_____

_____

_____

_____

3. How does what we go through help us grow and develop passion to ignite hope in others? Can you share why you think that?

_____

_____

_____

_____

_____

_____

4. My story of contagious courage and the ability to rise and shine illustrates that much sacrifice and discipline is required. However, that alone isn't enough. What did you note from my discoveries to be the key element to make it possible to "rise and shine?"

_____

_____

_____

_____

_____

_____

(a) Are there distractions that are keeping you from making prayer a priority in your life? Can you acknowledge them?

_____

_____

_____

_____

_____

_____

(b) Another important question as you acknowledge any distractions is: what are you willing to change so you don't leave out that key ingredient? I pray that you grasp the truth that you, too, can experience what it means to *Rise and Shine!*

_____

_____

_____

_____

_____

_____

Wow, we have covered a lot of ground! And, you might feel overwhelmed. However, I hope you can see how to use this assessment to monitor and track your ongoing progress. You will be able to pinpoint any areas that you may need to work on when you don't know where to begin. But also, I trust you'll be able to see areas of growth that will empower you to have the courage to move forward. Remember: keep moving through the different areas at your own pace and you *will* grow stronger with a clear path forward.

My relationship with my Heavenly Father has become and continues to be essential for me for each step I take. However, I *have* also included other steps that have been part of my experience as I have grown and continue to grow in courage and freedom. Maybe your first step is seeing a counselor or a doctor. Maybe it's having a long overdue conversation with a friend or family member. It might even be having a long overdue conversation with God as you acknowledge your disapproval of how He has handled your situation. It might even be that you finally forgive yourself so you can let the chain of shame or guilt break off of you.

Even the slightest step forward in His direction will be meaningful. Maybe you are unsure about trusting God to be that focal piece of your life. My advice would be to consider it like a first date or something. Go into it with an open mind. Ask your questions, but then be willing to listen. No pressure or obligation. He is a gentleman and will lovingly wait for you until you are ready. But either way, I want to help you figure out where to begin or encourage you to keep going forward if you get stuck or overwhelmed. Whatever that first step is, *you can find the courage to take it!*

Battle For Endurance

As you reflect on all the things you have just experienced on our journey here together, I want to leave you with some final thoughts about what I have learned that helps me maintain my courage and freedom—now more than ever. And, I hope it helps you in yours.

At the beginning of 2020 I chose two words that were going to be "my words" to declare or embrace for the year. They were *discipline* and *endurance*.

These two words have really made an impact in my life this year as I had to adapt to the COVID-19 pandemic. After a few weeks into this "new normal" for our world, I remember getting really excited to create some positive online content. On one particular day I showed a 20-minute video that had taken me 3 days to prepare, record, and edit. When only 3 people showed up to watch, my first reaction was, of course, disappointment. For a moment I even wondered *what's the point*, am I wasting my time? And before I even made it back upstairs from my little recording studio, God spoke these words into my heart. "I would have gone to the cross for *one*."

And with that, I was reminded about the mentality I began my ministry with. I've always believed, "If what I do touches even one person, it is worth it." Before this pandemic, the amount of people who responded to my content had never mattered. Why now, after 4 years of speaking, blogging and posting, am I being affected this way? Why? And I realized the reason: I had started making decisions about my on-line presence based on what "I" thought was best (or some self-imposed "comparison pressure" I was feeling) rather than on what God had in mind and even assigned for me to do.

God said, *"Vahen, keep leading with your heart and don't get in your* head. Resist striving in your own strength or according to your preconceived ideas." He continued by saying, *"It doesn't matter what you post as long as you are sharing from your heart. If in a year from now you are still in the pandemic and being forced into isolation, people will need to see the joy you have more than any well-put-together performance. So, if anything attacks your endurance in this season, let it go. Your joy will be the best thing you can offer people who are losing hope. Having the discipline to stay close and show that the joy of the Lord is your strength will be the message that will never lose its effect."* That word spoke into my heart that day rings louder now as I write this, than even on the day it was first given.

I realize now that although the things I do out of obedience to Him may take a lot of work, the moment something affects my endurance or makes me want to quit, it's time to discern where that is coming from. If the overload is because of self-imposed comparisons or something I've taken on that the Lord had not assigned, that is when "letting go" becomes my obedient response to Him. I knew God was teaching me to have endurance in a way I had not yet understood.

It's not always easy to discern if something is a hindrance to your endurance or a struggle presented to strengthen or prepare you for an assignment. Because, if I am honest, my default was always that if it's too hard or uncomfortable, "let it go" and that is not healthy. If you're always running from a struggle you can't grow. For example, remember that Hope conference I tried so desperately to "let go" of? Pressing through helped build my endurance. This opposition was definitely an opportunity for growth. The real takeaway was that God was increasing my capacity.

When people want to know how I have learned to discern which response is pleasing to the Lord, I tell them I begin my day with God. And during my day, if there is anything that threatens my endurance or tempts me to quit, I immediately go back to Him to direct me. Even that has been a hard skill I to learn.

There is a new cycle that I've adopted that has helped me to sustain my endurance: *fight, retreat, rest, refresh, and repeat.* I am more aware than ever that I need to be disciplined to cycle through these stages and go through them more rapidly than I had before. Staying in one stage too long will prove harmful to maintaining my endurance. My endurance of patience. Endurance of peace. My endurance of joy. Knowing when to sit and rest or say "no" is just as important as knowing when to run and fight the battles that are raging around us. If you get tired physically or restless in your spirit and you are tempted to give up the fight, *stop, retreat, rest, refresh and repeat.*

Understanding this is a *journey* of endurance not a *sprint* has proven most beneficial. Protecting my endurance in all the areas of my life continues to be so important.

While learning to build my endurance by going back to God with everything I was feeling, a very real lie of the enemy was exposed. The enemy tried to make me feel that God was *bothered* by all the times I would need Him. That lie would try to consume my attention especially if in the middle of the day I felt the need to just go and throw myself on the bed and cry out in prayer asking God to hold me. No words other than "I'm hurting; please hold me." Just the simple act of going to Him about the little things was even more important than running to Him for the big things. But do you know what the enemy would be saying? "There you go—running to God again." I can't explain it other than to say he was trying everything he could to *keep me away from God*. But when I started to really see the strength and courage I would gain from being in His presence, fear had no more control over me. That accusing and belittling voice was silenced.

I remember my breakthrough day well. That was the day God helped me reject the lie that I was *bothering* Him. He spoke into my heart, "How many times do you call your mom?" Some days I would lose count of how many calls we made back and forth to each other. Day or night. Anytime. Mom would always pick up the phone. God helped me see that I could come to Him just as often and as much as I needed because He is always there, too. "And even if you don't need anything," He said, "I want you to come and just sit with me." As a result, He is now my dear friend.

How are you handling the struggles of life? Are you overwhelmed or losing your endurance to keep going? I would like to challenge you try my approach. My life is the evidence that it works. More importantly, a relationship with God works.

I can't help but think of this endorsement by Jeremiah Raible regarding *Contagious Courage*. He said, *"Contagious Courage is going to be a great tool and an inspiration for so many. Because of Vahen's "never give up, never back down" attitude, she takes away the millions of excuses that people have about why they can't do X,Y or Z. Each person that reads Contagious Courage will come face to face with the challenge to take the next step. Imagine if millions of people had contagious courage—that's what I see happening as a result Vahen's book, Contagious Courage."*

When I was at youth camp "back in the day," they taught us this phrase about the impact of influencing one person. It went like this with my simple spin at the end: "If every 'one' won 'one,' and every 'one' who won 'one,' won 'one,' then every 'one' would have contagious courage." It's a tongue-twister and kinda silly, but I think you get my point.

My last and final thought as I leave you is this. I pray that as you reflect on my life's journey, you'll note many lessons learned similar to yours. But even more than that, I pray you see how *your* courage can become contagious. And one day (maybe even *today)* as you share your lived through experiences with others you meet, your life and your words will make it in someone else's survival guide. You will begin to not only see, but truly experience, *Contagious Courage*.

Resources

1. CornerBend Ministries - Grief Education: www.cornerbend.com

2. Cornerstone Counselling: www.cornerstonecounselling.com

3. Crossroads 24/7 Prayer Line: (1-866-273-444)
   www.crossroads.ca/247prayer/

4. Disability Education: www.andreafoster.ca

5. Freedom Session: www.freedomsession.com

6. Going Farther: www.goingfarther.org

7. Little Warriors Be Brave Ranch: www.littlewarriors.ca

8. National Hope Talks: www.nationalhopetalks.com

9. ReYu Paralysis Recovery Centre: www.reyu.ca

10. Spinal Cord Injury Canada: www.sci-can.ca

11. YouVersion Free Bible App: www.bible.com

Recommended Books

1. Mark Batterson: *All In – You Are One Decision Away From a Totally Different Life*

2. Connie Jakab: *Bring Them Closer – Calling Parents to Courage through the Mental Health Crisis*

3. Peggy Kennedy: *Chosen – Conversations of God with His Mighty Warrior*

4. Bruce Wilkinson: *The Dream Giver – Following Your God-Given Destiny*

5. Priscilla Shirer: *Gideon – Your weakness. God's strength.*

6. Vahen King: *Going Farther – Experience the Power and Love of God That Turns Tragedy into Triumph*

7. Shirley Thiessen: *The Little Black Funeral Dress – Five Things I Wish I Had Known About Grief*

8. John & Laura King: *OFF THE WALL & On His Pedestal – Escapades of a Maverick Missionary*

9. Robert S. McGee: *The Search for Significance – Seeing Your True Worth Through God's Eyes*

10. Ruth Haley Barton: *Strengthening the Soul of your Leadership*

11. Lisa Bevere: *Strong: Devotions – To Live a Powerful & Passionate Life*

12. Glori Meldrum: *Warrior – From surviving child sexual abuse to building the first world-class treatment centre for kids who have been sexually abused*

13. Bob Jones: *You're Going To Be OK – Real Hope For Fighters of Cancer, Mental Illness, Sexual Abuse or Loss*

Other Titles by Vahen King

Going Farther:

Experience The Power and Love of God That Turns Tragedy into Triumph

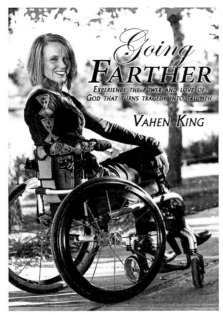

This is a powerful story of one woman's journey through deep emotional, physical, and spiritual pain - one of inspiration and courage. Transverse myelitis almost took her life, her marriage and her faith in God, but get ready to experience the power and love of God, that turns a litany of tragedies into miraculous triumph! You will laugh, cry, hope, and pray with Vahen as she meticulously weaves the story of God's love and grace into the fabric of her life. This is a story of courage and devotion that will inspire and challenge you to go farther.

Acknowledgments

When can I read your book?" Those six words planted seeds into my heart back in 2012 that grew to enable me to present to you with book #2! It's hard to believe that even when I thought a first book was nearly impossible, here we have the second.

So many people have encouraged me and believed in me throughout this book writing process and I am very grateful to them. My editor and dear friend, Peggy Kennedy, has made this writing *process* seem less like a "process" to get through, but rather an opportunity to empower and encourage me along the way.

To all my friends and family, I appreciate your understanding and support to get this message out. I cherish all the times you have graciously lent me your ear as you became my captive audience. Sharing concepts, brainstorming new ideas, or simply letting me vent, cry, or rejoice as I worked my way through this growing process. You know who you are. Your love and support mean so much to me.

Mom, you are my biggest cheerleader. You tell me that your dream is now to help your children fulfill their dreams. What more could a daughter ask for? No one will know the countless hours we have spent laughing, crying, and praying together. I've definitely had your ears and shoulders more than anyone. And to Mom King, your unwavering belief in me and the message of contagious courage has also been such a huge blessing. You are a "silent partner" who I am proud to acknowledge.

My amazing husband, my prince charming Vaughan: my heart is overflowing with love as I recall our journey. Together we have faced mountains and giants, yet we have come through to the other side standing stronger than ever. Because of your God-given strength and courage to hold onto me, I have a story to share. You are the best travel companion a gal could ask for. I refer to our relationship like that of flying a kite. Thank you for keeping me grounded but still letting me fly!

Thank you, Abigail Pond McKenna, for allowing me to include your drawing of *'Too Much Noise'* in chapter 7. When I first met you in that youth night zoom call, I saw that you were not only a talented young woman, but that you have a very powerful story to tell through your drawings!

I'm also happy to acknowledge my brother in-law Lance King. His artistry surfaces in chapter 22, *'Turtle on a post'.* Lance, you have such a crazy talent to bring things to life through your drawings. And I wish Father John, who was the master at enabling people to rise and shine, was here to see all this unfold. He would be so proud. I wish he could be here to share in these special moments, but Lance, I thank you for letting me use your talent to share my heart.

I also want to acknowledge my late father in-law, John King. The writing style of *Contagious Courage* was inspired by him. He was a great storyteller and was always pushing people to think outside of their comfort zones to experience a bigger bolder life. In his book titled: *Off The Wall & on HIS Pedestal*, he expresses his missionary life experiences with wit and humor. It was as if you were reading his diary. While I don't claim to be a master storyteller as he was, my desire has always been to share stories from my heart to yours, sprinkled with a few laughs along the way. I trust these chapters will challenge and empower you to step outside the limitations of your "comfort zone."

And, to you, the reader: I thank you for taking the time to sit with me and consider your own journey of contagious courage as I take you on mine. It is my prayer that these stories encourage you and that the principles they express help you see that freedom and contagious courage can also be your reality.

I am so blessed that we are already seeing the spread of contagious courage. The recent Kickstarter campaign success was just another of the many ways made evident, so thank you to all who contributed. Please refer to the special thanks section next to see all the people who pledged.

Special thanks to all the people who have blessed me with their empowering endorsements for this book. I am humbled and blessed to have such amazing champions of courage in my corner. I love and respect you all. I have been amazed at the times of "breakthrough" as the writing progressed. I thank the Lord for these reminders that He really was the one who called me to this assignment. I also am aware that breakthroughs would not have come without the earnest commitment of my intercessory team. Thank you for your strategic intercession at each phase of this journey. Your prayers have protected the process and will continue to guard His purposes.

Contagious Courage was birthed as a result of faith, obedience, and a disciplined ear tuned to the heart of my Heavenly Father. So most of all, I want to thank Him, because as I did my part He did '...exceedingly abundantly above all that I could ask or think...' (Ephesians 3:20) As I share what He's spoken into my heart, I pray He will speak into yours. It is because of Him and His strength in me that I have CONTAGIOUS COURAGE!

Special Thanks

I want to give a HUGE thank you and shout out, to the following supporters (and to those who chose not to be recognized publicly), for believing and backing the kickstarter campaign for this Contagious Courage book. I greatly value your contribution to help support the mission to spread hope and contagious courage. We are partners together!

— A —
Faith Anderson

— B —
Doreen Baker
Christine Ball
Sandy & Anne Bath
Kellie Bessey
Pastor Velemer & Irene Bessey
Jeanette Best
Susan Bourelle-Rattai
Ruth Boyde
Krystal Brooks
James H. Brown

— C —
Victoria Caison
Doris Chaput
Charity
Harvey & Gloria Conway

— D —
Chelsey & Brooklyn (Little Miss Wheelchair Canada) Denommee
Jill Didow
Kirby & Rosemarie Duzan

— E —
Erica Egedy (Sister)
Justin, Kelly, Gemma & Oliver Elford
Clint & Valerie Ellard

— F —
Andrea Foster
Adrienne Fudge

— G —
Melanie Gibson
Michelle Gillett Harris
Evelyn Goodyear

— H —
Angela Hancharyk
Michelle Hlady
Pastor Doug & Diane Hnatiuk
Barbara Hutchings

— I —
Pastor Eric & Susie Ings (Mom & Dad)
Carl, Lorraine, Bryanna & Catherine Ings (Brother)

— J —
Darlene Jefferise
Bob and Jocelyn Jones

— K —
Craig & Chelsea Kalvin
Lance & Jillian King & family
Laura King (Mother-In-Law)
Pleman King
Vaughan King (Husband)
Sarah Krygsman

— L —
Sidney Luther

— M —
Delores Mackey
Louise Mah
Holly Mascioli
Samantha McLeod
Eleanor and Ean McMillan
Kathleen Mouland
Mychela

— N —
Ed & Karen Nichols

— O —
Linda O'Reilly

— P —

Christine Pardy
Pamela Parker
Fern Penny
Clement & Danielle Phung
Terralyn Polege
Bob & Yvonne Prentice
Jonathan & Tamara Prosser & family

— R —

Sarah Ragoonath
Jeremiah & Kathy Raible
Irene & Randy Rennick

— S —

Patricia Saunders
Larry & Marleen Scarbeau
Kevin Shepherd
Jaime Smith
Saundra Somerville
Sarah Srdarev
Sudhar & Mary Jaya Stanislus
Jocelyn Stokes
Edna Stubbington
Ian Sturek
Brenda Sturge

— T —

Debra Teichgraber
Shirley Thiessen

— V —

Linda Valentine
Cheryl Vincent

— W —

Leann Woelk

— Y —

Garry & Lexie Young

About The Author

Vahen King is an author, speaker and founder of the non-profit charity, Going Farther. In 2017, Vahen was crowned the first ever Miss Wheelchair Canada and went on to win the prestigious title of Miss Kindness World. Showing not only her beauty, but her character has won her awards.

In 2019, Vahen was featured at International Day For Persons with Disabilities as someone who is not only making a difference in her community, but also as someone who isn't allowing her disability to limit her personal or professional success. Vahen story motivates not only those with disabilities, but anyone who has had to overcome struggles, or needs to be encouraged.

Vahen's courage is contagious. She inspires boldness and resiliency by facing each new adversity head-on. She demonstrates that the biggest limitations or disabilities are often the ones we place on ourselves.

At the age of 23, one week after her engagement to the man of her dreams, Vahen developed Transverse Myelitis, a virus that left her physically disabled and dependent on the use of a wheelchair. Although Vahen portrayed confidence as she was trying to cope as a person with a disability, her "new normal" was facing feelings of self-doubt and exclusion. Reaching a point of desperation, she realized that she had a choice to make: to be paralyzed by fears and insecurities, or push forward.

Vahen states, "While Transverse Myelitis set me on a path I would never have chosen, it has led me to find the strength and courage I didn't know existed, and actually brought me into the fulfillment of my wildest dreams."

Through the ministry work of her organization, Vahen plans to continue to reach out to as many people as possible and use her contagious courage as a platform of hope. From that platform she is igniting hearts with hope, while empowering and equipping them to go farther than they ever dreamed.

Vahen currently lives with her amazing husband Vaughan, in Edmonton, Alberta, Canada, and considers it a true honor and privilege to share her story of hope and courage with the world.

Stay Connected

Vahen would like to invite you to stay connected with her and be a part of her journey as she spreads the message of hope and courage to the world around her.

Visit goingfarther.org to;
- Invite Vahen to speak or host a conference or webinar
- Subscribe to Vahen's blog to receive the latest news, praise reports, speaking dates, new publications and more

For more inspiration and hope, follow Vahen on all her social media platforms:
- Facebook: facebook.com/GoingFarther.org
- Instagram: instagram.com/vahenking/
- YouTube: youtube.com/c/VahenKingContagiousCourage
- Twitter: twitter.com/vahenking
- Linkedin: linkedin.com/in/vahenking-goingfarther

Share Your Thoughts

In the beginning of this book Vahen encouraged you to journal your thoughts. If you have done that and would like to share an 'aha' moment of how *Contagious Courage* has impacted your life, you can send link to a short 3 min video, or a paragraph or two to info@goingfarther.org. Vahen would love to hear from you. Your story *could* be featured in a her monthly blog, Contagious Courage interview, or on social media as a testimony of how the message of *Contagious Courage* is changing lives.

Also, if you enjoyed this book, Vahen would love to encourage you to take a moment to review it on Amazon and/or Goodreads. Every positive review helps further this book's reach into other peoples lives. Thank you!